The Modern Irish Draught

by

Nicholas O'Hare

Harkaway
Ireland

The author wishes to acknowledge the assistance of breeders and owners who provided details of their animals without which this book would be an incomplete record

Front cover photograph Crosstown Dancer
courtesy Anne Hughes and Suma Stud

First Published 2002
ISBN 0-9541310-2-9

Other Books by Nicholas O'Hare
King of Diamonds
The Irish Sport Horse

Printed and bound by Antony Rowe Ltd, Eastbourne

Foreword

The purpose of this book is to present a review of the Irish Draught as it is today. Hopefully readers will be able to use it give themselves an overview of the existing Irish Draught world without too much historical baggage. Hopefully also the book provides adequate if brief sketches of the stallions, mares and competing horses with which it deals. The object is to provide information which might not be easily available elsewhere.

The main body of the book deals with the scene in Ireland and for the purpose of readily identifying modern pedigrees has been divided into six sections identified by the mainstream stallions which have contributed to the make-up of the breed as it is in 2002. These stallions are King of Diamonds, Clover Hill, Pride of Shaunlara, Ben Purple, and the less numerous but important families of Laughton and Slievenamon.

King of Diamonds traced back to Young JP (12) on his sire side. His dam pedigree was mixed although his dam Ruby was by Trueboy a halfbred sire who in fact traces back to Kildare (40). The grand dam was a thoroughbred mare called Biddens. Clover Hill was by the thoroughbred racehorse Golden Beaker but his dam was a mare by Tara who traced back to Young JP. Pride of Shaunlara by Milestone traced back to Young JP on the sire side. His dam was Boston Burglar by the thoroughbred Prefairy. Ben Purple traced back to Young JP on both sides. The Laughton line is a modern one created by the Hodgins family on a thoroughbred foundation. Slievenamon was the grandson of a thoroughbred but the sire of his dam, Rusheen Hero, carries Young Arthur (9) and Young JP in his pedigree. Thus the Irish Draught in Ireland is dominated by the influence of these six stallions. The situation in Britain is slightly different. There appears to have been a more conscious effort to retain outcross bloodlines there but the pressure is on for performance and I have no doubt that King of Diamonds, Clover Hill and Pride of Shaunlara bloodlines will dominate the entire Irish Draught world in the years to come. It may well be that breeders will have to go outside the studbook to introduce new blood which will provide a broader genetic base and offer greater ability.

Many breeders complain of the apparently irresistable performance factor which is now driving the breed, but it must be realised that there is no future for colder horses. The days of the horse in draught have gone and the owners of the future will require riding horses which can perform in all the disciplines. The challenge for Irish Draught breeders will be the retention of bone, substance and temperament in the more athletic horses of the future. The closing chapter expresses a personal belief that the breed does not currently encompass sufficient performance to allow it to survive There is I believe a case for reintroducing thorougbred blood to provide both increased genetic diversity and the degree of performance which will give the Irish Draught a more competitive edge.

While much of the book is devoted to breed stallions, there are chapters on special mares and accounts of important competing horses. I have dealt with the overseas scene as best I can from a distance. I wish to thank all those who corresponded with me and provided information about their horses without which the book could not have been prepared.

Contents

Contents

Contents

Contents

Contents

Contents

Early Days

The Irish Draught that we know today owes its existence to a decision by the Department of Agriculture in 1918 to open an Irish Draught Horse Studbook. Pressure to do so had been exerted by interested horse breeders for a number of years, notably by Patrick J. Hanlon, of Castleforth, in Co Carlow whose efforts led to an unsuccessful attempt to launch a studbook in 1911. He campaigned for the preservation of a type of horse which although used for ordinary farm work was unique to Irish soil.

Although Clydesdales had been imported to undertake a great deal of Irish agricultural work, the soil conditions and other environmental factors had led to the development of a lighter type of working horse which could be used under the plough, in harness and for ordinary riding and hunting. Their diversity to a large extent came from the fact that they were not a fixed breed. They were a light draught in contrast to the heavier agricultural horses of other countries and had crosses of thoroughbred.

Because of this many breeders did not consider them a breed at all, rather a type. The argument as to whether the Irish Draught was a type or a breed continued right down to the last quarter of the twentieth century, but now the Irish Draught, by virtue of the fact that it has been recorded in a studbook for over eighty years, has taken its place amongst the established horse breeds. The name Irish Draught is said to have been coined by dealers who came to buy horses for the English market.

In the years when Patrick Hanlon was pressing for registration, these horses were types, indeed they sometimes varied in relation to the parts of the country in which they were bred, but they were distinguished by an ability to perform in the disciplines of the day. Towards the end of the twentieth century the breed had adapted to some extent to the demands of showjumping and other equestrian sports.

The Irish Draughts of the late nineteenth and early twentieth century were descended from old Irish stock which had existed throughout the country, evolving from a melting pot of work horses and various kinds of saddle horses. Ireland had been renowned for centuries as a source of military horses which could handle all kinds of terrain and Irish breeders had a steady trade in supplying the purchasing commissions of almost every European army. Standards, however, had deteriorated, and the Westminister Government in the 1890's introduced a premium stallion scheme which aimed at improving matters by the approval and registration of thoroughbred stallions to cover the mares of the countryside at fees which the tenant farmers could afford.

The premium stallion schemes continued for a number of years, influencing the production of horses throughout the country, and when the inspectors came to register for the new Irish Draught book, many of the horses so inspected had been bred from crosses of thoroughbred blood. This influence in the backbreeding has been the source of much of the performance and quality which is found in the Irish Draught of today.

Horses with thoroughbred blood were admitted to the studbook up until comparatively recent times if they conformed to Irish Draught type. The successful producer of jumpers Clover Hill, a son of the thoroughbred racehorse Golden Beaker, is a case in point. The Irish Draught Horse Society introduced a scheme in 1989 whereby part bred fillies were admitted to an Appendix (AID) to the register. Their progeny by Irish Draught sires were eligible for inspection and full registration. The Appendix closed in 1992, but under pressure from falling numbers, the IDHS has re-opened the studbook in another limited way.

Serious Effort

In 1917 the Department of Agriculture decided to make a serious effort to permanently revive the breeding of Irish draught horses. Inspections were held and applications were received in respect of 1180 mares and 270 stallions, indicating a widespread belief that an indigenous breed did in fact exist. Following the inspections 375 mares and 44 stallions were passed as sound and suitable for entry in the new Irish Draught Horse Studbook.

Three leading experts of the day were appointed as inspectors. They were James Clarke, Navan, Co Meath, Patrick Shelly, Callan, Co Kilkenny, and P.J. Howard, MRCVS, Ennis, Co Clare.

They reported: "In making our selections of mares, we adopted a good average standard of merit, and were particularly careful to exclude mares showing signs of coarseness or signs of imported cart-horse blood. No well made mare that could be regarded as a good, useful farm animal of the clean legged draught type was passed over without careful consideration.

Foundation Stock

"Taken as a whole, the mares which we have recommended for entry in the Book are a good lot of animals, which can be regarded as an excellent foundation stock for establishing a breed of clean-legged draught horses really suitable to the requirements of the average Irish farmer.

"With regard to the stallions, in making our selections we set a high standard of merit, and we have not recommended for entry any sires respecting which there was a reasonable doubt in our minds, either on the score of general merit, or in the matter of pedigree. Our main concern was to choose animals having, in the first place good general conformation; and, secondly, true Irish Draught character and weight. In considering the question of breeding, we have been most careful to exclude such sires as had imported cart horse strains so far as we could trace. We were not so strict in regard to Thoroughbred blood, and we have recommended a few sires which have one or two crosses of Thoroughbred more or less remote in their pedigree. With these exceptions the selected sires come from old strains of Irish Draught horses.

"The question of action also received considerable attention, and whilst we did not look for anything in the nature of extravagent, we satisfied ourselves that the horses we selected were reasonably straight and true movers. We are very pleased to be able to report that taken as a whole, the sires which we have recommended for entry in the Book are excellent stud animals, and we are convinced that, regarded as clean-legged draught sires, they could not be equalled by horses imported from any other country. They are distinct in type and pre-eminently suited to Irish conditions.

"All the selected animals, both mares and stallions, were subjected to a strict veterinary examination prior to their being recommended for entry in the Book.

"We have given careful thought as to the prospects of access of this scheme. In the course of our work we were constantly in touch with persons interested in the horse breeding industry, particularly those who were keen on animals of the Irish Draught type. In so far as it rests with those people, we believe that they will permit in supporting the scheme and will breed from animals entered in the Book, provided that stallions will be placed within reasonable distance of mare owners. This is a matter of vital importance, and we strongly recommend the Department to spare no pains or expense in arranging an equitable distribution of the available sires. Should this be done, and should a general policy in regard to this scheme, similar to that adopted in 1917, be followed in future years, we are confident that the success of the scheme is assured, and that in time there will be in the country a distinct breed of clean-legged draught horses, which could not be excelled, and in sufficient numbers to supply the demand now existing for a heavier class of sire."

Distinct Breed

At a distance of more than eighty years it can now be seen that the aspirations of the inspectors have been achieved. There is indeed in existence a distinct breed. That it has so evolved is down not just to the goodwill of the Department who maintained the studbook over that period but to the self help attitude of Irish Draught breeders who in the late 1970s founded the Irish Draught Horse Society which has done so much to bring the breed into the twentyfirst century. The purpose of the Irish Draught has changed. The breed is no longer required to work the land or drive to the creamery, and it is as a saddle horse, and indeed to some extent as showjumper that the Irish Draught has evolved. Its days under the plough have passed. The question for the future is will the Irish Draught be truly successful as a riding and competition horse.

The Department of Agriculture published Volume 1 of the Irish Draught Horse Book in 1918. In a wide ranging introduction the Department referred to the fact that the "first authentic reference to the Irish Draught horse dates from the close of the eighteenth century. At that time a great increase in the area of land under tillage took place, and this created a demand for a bigger, stronger, and more docile horse than was required when the land was chiefly devoted to the rearing of flocks and herds. Though there are historical references to the importation at this period of draught horses from England to meet this demand, we have reason to believe that these horses failed to serve the purpose for which they were intended.

"The prejudicial influence of the cross of the heavy cart horse on the Irish mare seems to have been recognised even at this early period. The cross was found unsuitable, and the effort to effect improvement in this way was eventually abandoned. The people, were therefore, compelled to rely on the selection of the heavier of their native horses for the production of animals of a type suitable for farm work.

"The animal produced in this manner must have been a farm horse of good quality; for he filled that position when Ireland was largely engaged in tillage; he was also a roadster of sufficent merit to suit the requirements of a farming population, and though too coarse for hunting he had a natural liking for the sport, as shown by his high spirit and the readiness with which he took to jumping. One of the most valuable characteristics of the Irish Draught horse was its suitability for mating with the Thoroughbred. To this cross we owe the Irish hunter, which has established for Ireland a worldwide reputation.

"The great demand for Irish hunters and their increasing value, as years passed by, resulted in their widespread and general production. Given the Irish Draught mare to mate with the Thoroughbred sire, hunter breeding was simplicity itself. But when breeders were compelled to couple the Thoroughbred sires with mares of two or more crosses of Thoroughbred blood, the result became a matter of a good deal of uncertainty. The hunter being a cross bred animal, it is obvious that the maintenance of a definite type depended largely on the balancing of the two factors which produced him. But breeders were compelled, owing to the disappearance of the old draught type, to rely more and more on Thoroughbred blood. It is true that the best and most valuable hunter is the Thoroughbred, but the production of animals of this class is so very uncertain that it can never be recommended for general adoption. Apart from this consideration, the need of a hardy active horse for farm work became increasingly great as tillage revived.

"During the past fifty years Irish Draught horses have steadily decreased in number. The extension of tillage at the close of the eighteenth century was mainly responsible for their evolution; its decrease, especially during the last thirty years, is accountable for the present scarcity of these animals. The decrease in the area under tillage began on the larger farms, and by degrees the draught horses passed almost entirely into the hands of the smaller farmers. The agricultural depression which set in about 1879, and which continued up to recent times, so crippled the small farmers that they were compelled to part with their good colts and fillies. Consequently, after a drain of nearly forty years we are now left with comparatively few specimens of the breed. This must be regarded as a national loss.

Other Breeds Failed

"The disappearance of the Irish Draught horse left the small farmer and the hunter breeder with a common grievance: the one required an animal suitable for his farm work, the other needed something to give more bone and size to his brood mares."

Referring to the use of imported heavy breeds, mainly Shires and Clydesdales, the inspectors concluded: "Experience has, however, shown that these breeds have failed to fulfil the objects for which they were introduced. It is true that by importing more substance and strength to the progeny of the mares with which they were mated they have, by the production of an animal saleable at an early age, afforded temporary relief to the small farmer in some parts of the country, but they do not meet the requirements of the majority of Irish farmers who require and prefer a more active, clean-legged horse. Their use in the production of hunters has not been attended with any success, doubtless because these heavy breeds differ so widely from the Thoroughbred in conformation, temperament and breeding, that the two types cannot be satisfactorily interbred."

The Thoroughbred

The most relevant aspect of this account of the Irish Draught in the 150 years or so up to the establishment of the Irish Draught Book in 1918 is the continued reference to the Thoroughbred. The Thoroughbred is the great improver. Without him the Irish Draught, and indeed so many other breeds would not have quality and performance. The Thoroughbred is the key to performance in the Irish Draught.

The two great performance sires of modern times, King of Diamonds and Clover Hill, both had thoroughbred in the background, King of Diamonds further back, but Clover Hill quite close behind indeed. The Irish Draught would not have survived without its thoroughbred influences. It may well be that to meet the demands of the twentyfirst century which will exclusively focus on horse sports, the breed will have to look to the thoroughbred once more to give it the competitive edge that will be required to ensure its survival.

What did the Irish Draught look like in the early years? Richard Carden, a leading Co Tipperary breeder and stallion owner, who was also a member of the Royal Dublin Society's Stallion Registration Committee (the Society was entrusted with the registration of Premium stallions by the Westminister Government), published an article in 1907 describing the Irish Draught as it was prior to 1850. "As regards conformation they were a long low build of animal, rarely exceeding 15.3 or 16 hands high, with strong short clean legs, plenty of bone and substance, short backs, strong loins and quarters, the latter, however, drooping and inclined to be what is called "goose rumped", slightly upright shoulders, strong neck and smallish head. They had good straight and level action, without its being extravagent, and could trot, canter and gallop. They were also excellent jumpers and this is generally recognised as being in some measure the result of their having the strong peculiarly formed quarters mentioned above.

Carden went on to say: "No authentic information regarding their breeding is now available though no doubt many breeders carefully preserved the strain in their breeding herds for many years, but it may generally be accepted that the original breeding of the 'Irish Draught Horse' was the result of the cross of imported thoroughbred sires on the stronger well bred mares of the country, which later must have had an infusion of Spanish or Arabian blood in their veins.

Carden observed also: "It must not be taken that the words 'cart' or 'draught' imply that these horses were kept purely for agricultural purposes, or were in any way the same type of blood as what are known in England or Scotland at the present day as the Shire or Clydesdale, as there are many instances of which some of these 'Irish Draught Horses' proved to be the best hunters of their time."

Riding Shoulder

Hunting has been one of the great horse sports in Ireland and Britain for centuries. Irish hunters in times past and still today are highly prized. Irish horses have dominated the English show hunter circuit for decades. Ikey Bell who was one of the legendary huntsmen of his time, had this to say: "Firstly this breed of Draught horse had a riding shoulder, and grew no hair on the legs, standing anything from 15.2 to 16.2; he was long and low, short in the cannon bone, with fetlocks, pasterns and feet of quality; in fact, was the type of old fashioned weight carrying hunters. His lineage contained much of the best old lines of thoroughbred blood, and I have heard it stated that in most instances the tail female line traced back to the Thoroughbred mare.

"Many Irish Draught-bred hunters found their way to The Shires into such studs of weight carriers as those of Sir Albert Muntz and Gordon Cunard. Much care had been taken in breeding these Draught horse sires, and at Ballinasloe, for instance, in days gone by when judging them the judges would first place them on their looks, but before deciding on the prizes they had to perform certain tests. A ton of sand had to be gamely drawn from out of a sandpit, they would then be ridden over a high gate and be galloped.

"At Mullinavat in Kilkenny there was an old stone cross to which at the horse fair two rival owners of Draught stallions would at times tether them and let them fight, and the one which showed the greatest courage influenced the demand for his services."

Breed Standard

Today the Irish Draught Horse Society which was formed in 1976 and followed in 1979 by the establishment of the Irish Draught Horse Society (GB) has set its own standard for the breed.

Type and Character: The Irish Draught horse is an active, short shinned, powerful horse with substance and quality. Standing over a lot of ground, he is proud of bearing, deep of girth, strong of back, loins and quarters. He has an exceptionally strong and sound constitution, and is known for his intelligent and gentle nature and good sense. Height at three years old: stallions standing 16.0 hh and over, mares from 15.2 hh with good, clean flat bone.

Head: Good, bold eyes set well apart, wide forehead and long well set ears. Head should be generous and pleasant, not coarse or hatchet headed. The jaw bones should have enough room to take the gullet and allow ease of breathing

Shoulders neck and front: Shoulders should be clean cut and not loaded. Withers well defined, not coarse. The neck set on high and carried proudly, showing a good length of rein. The chest should not be too broad and beefy. The forearms large and generous, set near the ground. The cannon bone or shin, short and straight with plenty of clean flat bone. Being back of knee (calf knee) is forbidden in stallions and most undesirable in mares, ie should not slope forward from knee to fetlock. The bone never round or coarse, the legs should be clean and hard with a little silky hair at the back of the fetlock as necessary protection. In winter, the legs may become 'woolly' but the hair should never be stiff or coarse, and at no time growing down the front of the hoof. Pasterns strong and in proportion, not short and upright nor long and weak. Hooves should be hard and sound, not large and flat like a carthorse, nor boxy or contracted and there should be plenty of room at the heel.

Back, hindquarters, body and hind legs: the back strong and girth deep with strong loins and quarters, not forgetting the mares must have enough room to carry a foal. The croup to buttocks to be long and gently sloping, not short and rounded or flat topped. Hips not wide and plain, the upper thighs very strong and powerful and at least as wide from the back view as the hips. The second thighs long and broad and powerful like forearm and well developed. The hocks sound and generous and like the knees, set into a good short shin. Hocks should not be too wide apart or close together. They must not be bent or weak in any way but should be in a line with the buttocks to the heel. The cannon bone short and strong like the front leg or shin and not sloping forward or weak.

Action: Smooth and free but without exaggeration and not heavy and ponderous. Walk and trot straight and true with good flexion of the hocks and freeedom of the shoulders.

Colour: Any strong whole colour including greys. Obvious Clyde marking not permitted, i.e. bay with white legs above the hocks and knees.

Performance Testing

Inspection is still part of the registration process for the Irish Draught. The IDHS carries out mare inspections at two years of age, and the Irish Horse Board Co-op Approves stallions. A limited form of performance testing is part of the Approvals procedure. Colts are inspected from three years of age and subject to the usual conditions of conformation, movement and soundness. Marking is made in accordance with points for Type and presence (20); Pedigree (20); Conformation broken down into head (5) neck (5), shoulders withers (20) body (20) topline (20) hindquarters (20) forelimbs and feet (25) hind limbs and hocks (25); Movement: forelimbs (25) hind limbs (25) Athleticism (50); Temperament 20. The total mark is 300.

The performance testing aspect of the inspection can be carried out in two ways, open competition or centralised testing. Irish Draught stallions must accumulate a minimum of 10 points in competitions under the rules of the Showjumping Association of Ireland, or under the rules of Eventing Ireland 5 points or Dressage Ireland 20 points. Having gained its points the stallion will then undergo a full inspection.

Central performance testing is carried out at a specified location over a 10 to 12 weeks period. This system is primarily designed for Irish Draught stallions.

In the period 1995-2000 42 Irish Draught stallions were selected for performance testing, 32 completed the test and eighteen were Approved.

The inclusion of the jumping element as an integral part of the Approvals system has not been without its critics. Some breeders hold the view that stallions should be approved without the performance testing element. As late as 2000, the IDHS Breeding Committee recommended the dropping of the performance test and its replacement with an elite classification for those stallions which undertook it successfully. The Irish Horse Board, however, is not in favour of such a move. and more discerning breeders do not favour it either.

The historical perspective of the breed as outlined in the foregoing part of this chapter indicates that the Irish Draught traditionally had jumping prowess and for this reason there should in fact be no objection to performance being assessed. The real question is whether the breed is capable of meeting the demands of modern jumping requirements. The purpose of this book is to assess the capability of the breed in this regard.

King of Diamonds

Two stallions have dominated the Irish Draught world over the past twentyfive years and their prowess as producers of performance horses has introduced them to a wider sphere. These sires are King of Diamonds and Clover Hill. Both of them established themselves as sires of jumpers and indeed it is true to say that were it not for these stallions the world of the Irish Draught might have been a very small one indeed.

King of Diamonds, a Grade A showjumper in his day, albeit at a time when the tracks were vastly different to those which are built today, has established a remarkable dynasty in terms of descendant stallions and competing progeny. He focused world attention for a time on the Irish Draught as a performance breed. The World Breeding Federation for Sport Horses in its returns for the six years ending 1996 placed him seventh sire in the world by progeny achievement. Seventeen of his progeny were listed in the international showjumping performance table. He had over forty descendant stallion progeny on the Irish stallion register.

Not Purebred

We have already seen that the Thoroughbred was an important influence on the breed. Both King of Diamonds and Clover Hill shared in that influence. Technically neither of them were purebred Irish Draughts but the difference between King of Diamonds and Clover Hill is that with the King the thoroughbred was further back. Clover Hill carried it close behind. King of Diamonds was by **Errigal**, a son of

Silvermines, which was the traditional Irish Draught side of his parentage. His dam Ruby was by **Trueboy** a halfbred sire who in fact traces back to Kildare, a well known Irish Draught stallion at the beginning of the century.

The grand dam was a thoroughbred mare called Biddens. The King was owned by Tom O'Neill of Slyguff Stud on the Carlow-Kilkenny border, a long time veteran of the stud business who lived until well into his late nineties.

King of Diamonds was bred by Tom O'Neill. The pedigree was in the family. The sire of his dam, Trueboy, was bred by a cousin Jack O'Neill of Whitemount, Kells, Co Kilkenny. Slyguff Stud now run by Loftus O'Neill, built a reputation as a home for jumping sires. Side by side with King of Diamonds, Tom O'Neill stood Imperius, a thoroughbred producer of world class international jumpers. Today his son Master Imp carries on that tradition.

The halfbred Trueboy was a bay roan standing 16 hands and a half inch by the Irish Draught Castlebawn (103) out of a mare called Lady Warrior (44) by Warrior subsequently registered as Black Duke (35). The sire of her dam was Sir Henry (6) by Young Sir Henry by Old Sir Henry. Sir Henry's dam was by the thoroughbred stallion Defiance. Castlebawn was the son of Kildare (40) who was a famous Irish Draught stallion in the early 1900s.

Errigal, the sire of King of Diamonds was by a good Irish Draught sire Silvermines (348) out of a mare called Barogue (2987) by Irish Pearl (193). Silvermines traced back through **Galty Boy** (94) to Brehon Law (59) a son of Young JP, number twelve in the Irish Draught Book and the founder of the important Kildare and Brehon Law lines in Irish

Draught breeding. Silvermines' dam was Young Hunter (2444) by Kincora (169). He made no other major contribution to the Irish Draught scene apart from being the sire of Errigal. The sire of Errigal's dam Irish Pearl (193) was by a son of Kildare called Pride of Cork (88) foaled in 1919. Thus the record shows that Kildare, the leading sire of the early part of the century, appears on both sides of King of Diamonds pedigree.

Errigal was a chesnut horse who stood with E. J. Byrne at Park Stud, Tullow, Co Carlow. He was foaled in 1953 and produced four stallions for the Irish Draught Studbook. One of these was Slyguff Hero (574) a full brother of King of Diamonds bred a year earlier. Notice must be taken of Galty Boy (94) in Silvermines' pedigree. He stood in Co Limerick and bred a number of showjumpers including the international stars Limerick Lace and Snowstorm. Galty Boy out of a mare by Klondyke (41), and a son of Brehon Law, was widely hailed as a sire of jumpers in his day. The question must be asked, was he an important influence on King of Diamonds performance, more so perhaps than the Trueboy bloodline.

Prolific Sire

King of Diamonds established himself as a prolific sire following in the footsteps of his ancestor **Kildare** who produced seventeen Irish Draught stallions and was the sire of the dams of eleven registered stallions. He stood in Co Cork. He was a champion at Dublin Horse Show in 1920. King of Diamonds was a performance tested horse in the days when such a concept was entirely novel to the Irish breeding scene. Breeders were able to see him jumping at shows and soon were to see a remarkable procession of jumping progeny. The success that these achieved encouraged the authorities of the day to put more and more descendant sires of the King on the stallion register. It may now be right to question the wisdom of this policy. Not all these sires have proved successful, either in performance terms or in terms of conformation and quality.

King of Diamonds died in 1991 at the age of 29. At that point he had twenty one descendant stallions in the Irish Draught section of the stallion register. The demand for jumping ability by breeders and buyers was recognised. This bloodline could provide it. One of his progeny **Special Envoy** was ranked number four in the World Breeding Federation's league of jumpers. There were other highly successful contenders. The success of King of Diamonds perhaps only accentuated the realisation that such performance was scarce in the Irish Draught as a breed. Time has eclipsed King of Diamonds from the World Breeding Federation table and none of his stallion descendants has replaced him. Times and standards have changed.

Diamond Lad

Two of King of Diamonds stallion sons made a particular impact. These were Diamond Lad and Flagmount Diamond. Diamond Lad (695) bred from a Ben Purple mare Kildalton Countess (10180), a daughter of Billy Cotter's mare Enniskeane Countess, was started in Co Limerick by John Shorten and later went to Hugh Hennigan in Roscommon and established himself as a formidable producer of jumpers. He registered 623 foals altogether and became one of the most popular sires in Ireland. His long and fruitful career came to an end in 1996. He contributed three sons to the stallion register, Welcome Diamond (825), Creggan Diamond (755), and All the Diamonds, as well as three sport horse stallions.

Welcome Diamond (825) was bred by Tom Fitzmaurice out of a Legaun Prince mare called Welcome and stood initially with Stephen Russell in Kilkee, Co Clare. He later went to Dermot McCarthy in Cork. A grey standing 16.2 hh he was foaled in 1990. He won the Dublin Horse Show Irish Draught class in 2001.

Creggan Diamond left 308 registered foals and was bred from an Armada Star (556) mare Carrigroe Star (9153) He was bred by Patrick Keena and stood with Jan Keck, at Kylebrack, Loughrea Co Galway. Creggan Diamond was foaled in 1983. He was a Grade A showjumper and produced jumpers. He was a bay standing 16.2 hh

All the Diamonds foaled in 1995 was bred by Eugene Laheen, Co Galway and Approved in 2000. He stands with Jan Keck. The dam is Menlough Star by Silver Sam (639). Silver Sam foaled in 1969 was a son of Merrion (447) by Merville Prince (309). Menlough Star a 1991 mare was out of an AID mare Loan Star by the sport horse sire Rossa by Rosyth (TB). The third dam Maghera Peggy is by Boherbue. All the Diamonds has started out on a showjumping career. He was Approved in 2000.

Diamond Lad was the sire of Loganny Legend (ISH) who produced the 1990 gelding **Point Blank** bred by Leonard King, Castlewellan, Co Down. Point Blank is a son of international sporthorse star Cruising. He is a winning Grand Prix contestor in the USA ridden by Christian Currey. Double Diamond a 1992 gelding by Diamond Lad is ridden by Canadian Chris Delia. He is also a Grand Prix contender.

Flagmount Diamond

Flagmount Diamond (702) was a son of the influential mare Gowran Betty who bred three stallion sons. He was foaled in 1976 and was still alive in 2001, the time of writing.

Flagmount Diamond went to George Nesbitt at Ballybay, Co Monaghan and produced 756 registered foals. A daughter of Flagmount Diamond produced the successful **Diamond Cliff** who rose to Grade A in England in one season. Diamond Cliff a 1988 gelding by Golden Cliff (TB) was bred from Lindy Lou Diamond (ISH) by John Ryan Portlaoise, Co Laois. He has won international speed classes. His owners are Martin Walsh, Ballinakill, Co Laois, and Martyn Donoghue, Cheshire. He is ridden by John Whittaker.

Flagmount Diamond also produced the 1989 gelding **Hopes are High**, winner of the King George VI Gold Cup at Hickstead in 1999. He had a double clear round in the nations Cup at Dublin for Great Britain the same year. He was ridden by Nick Skelton. Hopes are High was bred by Michael Hughes, Madden, Co Armagh from Helena's Lass (ISH) by Cornelscourt (TB).

Flagmount Diamond contributed the successful stallion jumper **Crosstown Dancer** who was one of the leading performers in the new crop of stallions in the late nineties. He was twice champion Irish Draught stallion at Dublin Horse Show and was National Breed Show champion as well as being champion RID foal at Dublin Horse Show.

Bred by Fintan Branigan, Drogheda, Co Louth, Crosstown Dancer stands at Suma Stud in Co Meath, a remarkable nursery of Irish Draughts orginally based on **Pride of Shaunlara**. Standing seventeen hands Crosstown Dancer is a liver chesnut out of a Pride of Shaunlara mare called Tara Sky. He has 227 registered foals to date.

Mount Diamond Flag (852) foaled in 1994 was approved in 1998 following central performance testing. A bay son of Flagmount Diamond his dam Drumanespil Lady (10530) was a daughter of Lahinch, one of the three stallion sons of **Laughton** (446) who founded an important breed sire line with thorougbred back breeding. Lahinch who stood with Vincent Faughnan in Leitrim produced ten stallion sons. Mount Diamond Flag has 70 foals to date.

Drumri (849) is a bay son of Flagmount Diamond. His dam was Drumbar Queen, a daughter of Lakeview Pride (757) by Western Pride (704). She is a grand daughter of Skylark on the dam side. Drumri was foaled in 1991 and was bred by Tommy Gargan. He stands with David McKenna, Muff, Kingscourt, Co Cavan. He is a Grade D showjumper.

Three other descendant stallions of King of Diamonds have performance credentials. These are Flagmount King and Classic Vision who are both Grade A's, and Glidawn Diamond who has produced jumping progeny and stallion sons.

Glidawn Diamond's best known showjumping offspring is Coolcorran Cool Diamond, a 1989 sport horse stallion out of the ISH mare Bonmahon Belle by Bronti (ISH). He was bred by Francis Fitzgerald and is owned and ridden by Irish international rider Robert Splaine. Coolcorran Cool Diamond was on Ireland's winning Nations Cup teams at Lummen and Rotterdam in 2000 and on the Northern American Nations Cups tour which resulted in two victories for the Irish team.

Flagmount King (747) jumped to Grade A and became an international contender as well, jumping on the British junior team. He was able to produce a rate which allowed him to compete in speed classes. Foaled in 1981 he eventually went to stand with Denis Phelan at Mullinavat, Co Kilkenny. He was bred by Martin Brophy from his good mare Gowran Betty. He has 372 registered foals

Welcome Flagmount (857) is a 1996 grey son of Flagmount King. His dam Welcome (10515) was a daughter of Legaun Prince (660) by Milestone (498) Her dam was Bealacana Blackberry by Rusheen Hero (445). He was bred by Tom Fitzmaurice and is owned by Gabriel Slattery, Claremorris, Co Mayo. He was approved in 1999 following central performance testing.

Classic Vision (827) a son of Ginger Dick had a showjumping career and retired at Grade A. His dam was a Flagmount Diamond mare Lady Glen (10384). He stood initially with Jim and Richard McLoughlin, Co Down and then went to Trevor Badger in Co Westmeath. Classic Vision's dam Lady Glen was jumped up to Grade A by Edward Doyle. She produced another stallion, a full brother to Classic Vision, Glenbrae who stands in England.

Glidawn Diamond (754) is one of the stallion sons of Kildalton Countess. He was foaled in 1982. He stands with William Kennedy at Ballyard Tralee, Co Kerry. He had a showjumping career and has produced jumpers. His stallion son **O'Leary's Irish Diamond** owned by Jim Leary of Lamy, New Mexico, has been doing well at dressage in the USA.

Another son **KEC Double Diamond** foaled in 1996 has also been exported to the USA. His dam Ballyard Katie (11786) was by Creggan Diamond giving him King of Diamonds on both sides of his pedigree. The second dam was the AID mare Ballinorig Dolly by Dangan King (613) out of an ISH mare by Jab (TB).

The Irish Horse Board approved another stallion son for service in 2001. This is KEC Blue Jay Diamond (869) out of Grey Curragong (10604)by the Conqueror giving him King of

Diamonds on both sides. Bred by Anna Kennedy he is owned by her husband William Kennedy, Cahirwisheen Stud, Tralee, Co Kerry.

Today (2001) King of Diamonds has nine sons on the stallion register and eleven grandsons. There are six great grandsons and eleven stallions which have King of Diamonds on their dam side. As might be expected most of his stallion sons are aging. The youngest is King Henry foaled in 1983.

Bobin

Bobin (833) is a grey 1990 great grandson of King of Diamonds by Duleek Hero (760) a son of Ireland's Pride. Duleek Hero's dam was Springfield Star (10296) by Ben Purple (580). Bobin's dam was Bridgemount Daisy (10337) by Skippy (688) by Legaun Prince (660). Her dam was Carignafila Daisy (8469) who has no further pedigree recorded. Bobin a winner of the young stallion class at the National Irish Draught Show was bred and is owned by Charles Reilly. He stands with Brendan Glavin, Gort, Co Galway. He has 28 registered foals.

Castana

Castana (837) is a 1991 chesnut by Naldo (773) a son of Lahinch (558). His dam Diamond Lilla (10827) is a daughter of Diamond Lad (695) by King of Diamonds. Her dam is Sweet Colleen (10449) by Rathlin Star (707) out of Gay Colleen (8654). He was bred by Mr and Mrs I Hurst and stood with Francis Lafferty, Ballaghadereen, Co Roscommon. He has 34 registered foals.

Copper King

Copper King (742) is a 1978 chesnut son of King of Diamonds out of the Vinegar Hill (463) mare White Sand Moll (8956).

Vinegar Hill was by Mount Loftus (348) There is no dam line pedigree recorded for White Sand Moll. Copper King was bred by RC Scanlon and stands with Leonard and Jonathan Lucas, Killygordon, Co Donegal. He has 94 registered foals.

Corran Ginger

Corran Ginger (812) is a 1989 chesnut son of Ginger Dick (643) by Bell Laughton (578) out of the Battleburn mare Laughton Lass. His dam Diamonds Colleen is by Kingsway Diamond (736) a son of King of Diamonds. Diamonds Colleen is out of Carrow Colleen (7925) by St Isadore (559) He was bred by Jack Pertry and is owned by Robert Davis, Ballybofey, Co Donegal. He has 115 registered foals.

Cream of Diamonds

Cream of Diamonds (780) is a 1985 chesnut grandson of King of Diamonds by Kingsway Diamond, who was exported to New Zealand. Kingsway Diamonds dam was Bawnlahan Beauty. Cream of Diamonds' dam was April Lass (10324) by Skippy (688) who was exported to England. Skippy was a son of Legaun Prince (660) April Lass's dam was Carrowmore Daisy (6957) by Knocknagow (600). He was bred by Thomas Niland and stands with Patrick Kyne, Claregalway, Co Galway.

Crosstown Pride

Crosstown Pride (851) is a 1995 chesnut son of Crosstown Dancer, the showjumping son of Flagmount Diamond and a great grandson of King of Diamonds. His dam was Crosstown Lark (11442) by Lake View Pride (757) a son of Western Pride (704). Western Pride by Lisheen is the sire of the registered RID stallion Western Light. Crosstown Lark's dam was Garrybawn Lark (10889) by Skylark (627). He was bred by Fintan Branigan and is owned by him.

Diamond Clover

Diamond Clover (824) is a 1990 chesnut son of Clover Hill (665). His dam is Highlight Girl (10693) a daughter of King of Diamonds out of Highlight 2, a daughter of the thoroughbred Highland Flight. Her dam was Laughton's Belle (8558). He represents a combination of the two great jumping lines in Irish Draught breeding. Diamond Clover was bred and is owned by Wilfred Atkinson, Durrow, Co Laois. He has 221 registered foals. He is discussed more fully in the chapter on Clover Hill.

Diamond King

Diamond King (756) is a 1983 grey son of the Conqueror (725) by Flagmount Boy (683) and great grandson of King of Diamonds. Flagmount Boy's dam was Gowran Betty who bred three stallion sons. His dam was Carrigbawn Coleen (9418) a daughter of Ben Purple. out of Flirty Gertie (8028) by Gortlee (426). He was bred by Daniel J Crowley and stands with Jack McKinley, Dungannon, Co Tyrone. He has 175 registered foals.

Diamond Rock

Diamond Rock (761) is a 1979 grey son of King of Diamonds out of the Cushnahouna (471) mare Kilmanagh Coleen (7787) Kilmanagh Coleen was a daughter of a Galgorm mare. Diamond Rock was bred by Thomas Purcell and stands with Simon McCarthy, New Ross, Co Wexford. He has 190 registered foals.

Duleek Hero

Duleek Hero (760) is a 1983 grey grandson of King of Diamonds by Ireland's Pride. The dam of Ireland's Pride was Tullagh Ireland's Glory by Merrion (447). Duleek Hero's dam was Springfield Star (10296) a daughter of Ben Purple (580). He was bred by Michael Casey and stands with Thomas Niland, Balla, Co Mayo.

Finns Clover Inn

Finns Clover Inn (850) is a bay 1995 son of Clover Hill. His dam was Thunder Girl (11151), a daughter of Diamond Lad (696) by King of Diamonds. He is discussed in the chapter on Clover Hill.

Ginger Holly

Ginger Holly (820) is a 1989 chesnut son of Ginger Dick (643) by Bell Laughton (578) a son of Laughton (446) Ginger Dick's dam Laughton Lass was by the thoroughbred Battleburn, the sire of the famous Boomerang. Ginger Holly's dam is Westfield Lass (10315) a daughter of Flagmount Boy son of King of Diamonds. Her dam was Westfield Rose (9025) by Galtylara (548)

Golden Trump

Golden Trump (799) is a 1988 chesnut grandson of King of Diamonds by Diamonds are Trumps (711). Diamonds are Trumps was a daughter of Kildalton Countess. Golden Trumps' dam is Silver Hills (10631) a daughter of Clover Hill out of the Silverstone (656) mare Jalna (10307). He was bred by George Frend and stands with James Berney, Gorey, Co Wexford. He has 154 registered foals.

Home Rule

Home Rule (775) is a 1983 chesnut great grandson of King of Diamonds by The Conqueror (725) a son of Flagmount Boy, the first officially tested performance stallion. The process was instituted by Bord na gCapall which was the authority at the time. He was ridden by John Hall. Home Rule's dam was Glen Lass (10402) by Gold Coin (638) by the thoroughbred Autumn Gold. Glen Lass's dam was Dolly Dear 2 (6301) by Glen Lad (458). He was bred by Timothy Kelleher and stands with Donal Shine, Newmarket, Co Cork.

Ireland's Pride

Ireland's Pride (705) is a 1977 grey son of King of Diamonds out of Tullagh Ireland's Glory by Merrion (447) a son of Merville Prince (309). Tullagh Ireland's Glory was a daughter of Gort Polly by Irish Rebel. Ireland's Pride was bred and is owned by Timothy Carey, Castletowngeoghegan, Co Westmeath. He has 358 registered foals.

Its the Quiet Man

Its the Quiet Man (830) is a grey 1991 son of Clonfert (694) by Bawnlahan (585) Clonfert's dam was Cousin Rachel (6053) by Blarney Castle (409). The dam of Its the Quiet Man was Cappagh View (10716) by Mountain View. Her dam was Cappagh Grey, an AID mare by Ireland's Pride (705) a son of King of Diamonds. Its the Quiet Man was exported to the United States and returned to Ireland winning the Stallion class in Dublin before going to stand with Anthony Gordon, Ballina, Co Mayo. He is owned by Martha du Pont. He was bred by Thomas McCrann. He has eight foals registered in Ireland.

Jack of Diamonds

Jack of Diamonds (743) is a 1981 grey son of King of Diamonds. His dam was the show mare Bawnlahan Beauty (426) a son of Kenmare (291) Bawnlahan Beauty won the Greenvale Championship at Millstreet in 1978. Bawnlahan Beauty's dam was Pride of Bantry. There is no further recorded pedigree. Jack of Diamonds was bred by David Hatton and is owned by Roberta Hampton, Craigavon, Co Armagh. He has 92 registered foals.

Kildalton King

Kildalton King (714) is a bay 1978 son of King of Diamonds out of the prolific mare Kildalton Countess, a daughter of Ben Purple. Her dam was Enniskeane Countess (5990) Kildalton

Countess was bred by Kildalton Agricultural College and is owned by Maurice Cousins, Gorey, Co Wexford. He has 435 registered foals. Kildalton King produced the showjumper **Windgates King Koal**, a 1988 gelding out of a Prince Rois (TB) mare. He was bred by Laurence Pender, Enniscorthy, Co Wexford and is ridden by Edward Doyle.

King Henry

King Henry (778) is a 1983 grey son of King of Diamonds out of Tubber Beauty (6787) by the thoroughbred Tynwald. No dam pedigree is recorded. King Henry was bred by Patrick Duggan and stands with Turlough McNamara, Leitrim. He has 114 registered foals.

Ri an Domhan

Ri an Domhan (813) is a 1988 chesnut son o (752) by Rathlin Star (707) by Armada Star (566). Golden Warrior's dam was Kylebeg Lass (10236) by Bawnlahan (585) out of Cousin Rachel (6053). Ri an Domhan's dam was Inch Lady Fair (10392), a daughter of Flagmount Boy (683) by King of Diamonds. Her dam was Lisacreasig Lady (7771) by Glen Lad (458). He was bred by Timothy Kelleher and stood with James McMahon, Ennis, Co Clare. He has 83 registered foals in Ireland. He has been exported to the USA.

Silver Glider

Silver Glider (770) is a 1984 grey son of The Conqueror and great grandson of King of Diamonds. His dam was Carrigbawn Colleen (9418) by Ben Purple (580). He was bred by Daniel J. Crowley and stands with John McShane Dundalk, Co Louth. He has 238 registered foals.

Star Kingdom

Star Kingdom (856) is a 1994 grey son of Annaghdown Star

by King Elvis (708) a son of Pride of Shaunlara (636). His dam Ireland's Diamond (10008) is a daughter of King of Diamonds. The grand dam is Tullagh Ireland's Glory by Merrion (447). He was bred and is owned by Timothy Carey, Castletowngeoghegan, Co Westmeath. He was approved in 1999 following central performance testing. He has 10 registered foals.

The Conqueror

The Conqueror (725) was a grey 1979 son of Flagmount Boy (683) and grandson of King of Diamonds. His dam was Droumaloughlin Dolly (10248) by Wild Wave (560) a son of Gortlee (426). No further pedigree is recorded. He was bred by Denis Moynihan and stood at the end of his career with Fulton Buchanan, Letterkenny, Co Donegal. He had 255 registered foals

Westmeath Lad

Westmeath Lad (834) is a 1991 chesnut son of Kildalton Gold (774) a son of Merry Gold (644) by Lahinch (558). Kildalton Gold's dam was Kildalton Countess. Westmeath Lad's dam was Ireland's Diamond a daughter of King of Diamonds. Her dam was Tullagh Ireland's Glory by Merrion (447). He was bred and is owned by Timothy Carey, Castletowngeoghegan, Co Westmeath. He has 66 registered foals.

King of Diamonds produced fourteen part bred stallion sons, or Irish Sport Horse sires as they are classified as well as a number of descendant sport horse sires, but it is the jumpers he produced which really brought him fame.

King of Diamonds has left a remarkable legacy and exercises an extraordinary influence on Irish breeding. Up to 700 foals are produced each year by Approved King of Diamonds sire descendants. Well over 300 other mares with King of Diamonds blood produce foals as well. In years to come people will undoubtedly ask what was so special about King of Diamonds. The answer is his prepotency. He proved himself a singular sire of jumpers not just in the first generation but down the line. King of Diamonds will be recorded in the history of Irish sport horse breeding as a true foundation sire.

Some International Showjumpers by King of Diamonds

Charlton

Charlton a 1990 gelding by Cavalier Royale (Holst) out of the sport horse mare Kilkenny Diamond by King of Diamonds was a successful showjumper produced by Marion Hughes. He competed for Portugal ridden by Miguel Bravo and was subsequently sold for a reported £1M.

Diamond Express

Diamond Express was ridden for fourteen years by Francis Connors. He had a highly successful showjumping career and excelled in Derby and Speed classes. He died from a heart attack in 1997 at the age of nineteen.

Lismakin

The Irish Army jumper Lismakin, ridden by John Ledingham. Lismakin is by Master Imp (TB) out of Erkina Queen (ISH) by King of Diamonds. He has competed on Irish Nations Cup teams.

Lough Crew

Lough Crew was a long serving member of the Irish Army's jumping team and won many international competitions in the seventies and eighties. He was bred by Jim Finnegan, of Stoneyford, Co Kilkenny out of a mare by Battleburn, the sire of Eddie Macken's Boomerang. He was selected for numerous Nations Cup competitions.

Mill Pearl

Mill Pearl was bred by Noel C. Duggan, Millstreet, Co Cork and foaled in 1979. Ridden by Joe Fargis of the USA she won team silver in the Seoul Olympics. She has won many Grand Prix competitions. Her full sister Millstreet Ruby is a Grand Prix winner. She is leased to the Irish Army.

Millstreet Ruby

Millstreet Ruby is a 1984 mare by King of Diamonds out of the Thoroughbred mare Carran by Anthony. She was bred by Noel C. Duggan, Millstreet, Co Cork, and was ridden for the Irish Army by Capt John Ledingham. She won a series of international speed classes in 1999.

Royal Athlete

Royal Athlete is a 1987 gelding by King of Diamonds out of the Bahrain (TB) mare Trixie lady. He was bred by James Whitty, Borris, Co Kilkenny. He competes internationally for Switzerland ridden by Marcus Hauri. He won the Derby at Berne in 2000.

Royal Lion

Royal Lion foaled in 1972 was an Eddie Macken ride who captured the Irish puissance record of 7ft 3 inches at Dublin Horse Show in 1983. A l6.32 hh chesnut he was bought as a yearling by leading breeder and producer Patricia Nicholson who gave him to her daughter Suzanne as a twenty first birth day present. He was an outstanding jumper with a remarkable ability to faultlessly handle big fences.

Special Envoy

Special Envoy the long time mount of Brazilian rider Nelson Pessoa is unquestionably the front runner of King of Diamonds sporting progeny. Nelson Pessoa and more recently his son Rodrigo have made their mark on world showjumping. Abbeville and Vivaldi were amongst the top horses in the world. Pessoa senior after suffering a heart attack went back to win the Hickstead Derby for the third time on Vivaldi, a remarkably courageous feat. Special Envoy was placed fourth in the 1993 world rankings. He ranks with Eddie Macken's Boomerang as one of the greatest Irish showjumpers. The

Pessoas, father and son, achieved a remarkable double in 1995 when they partnered Special Envoy and Tomboy to win gold at the Pan American Games.

Vagabond King

Vagabond King is a 1984 gelding by KIng of Diamonds out of Carrigbrahan Betty (ISH) by Harrigan (TB). He was bred by John Connolly, Fenor, Co Waterford. He is an international Grand Prix winner ridden by W. Wauters, Belgium.

Clover Hill

The performance mantle of King of Diamonds was picked up by Clover Hill. The story of this stallion is the classic example of a sire with no individual performance credentials succeeding through the feats of his progeny. Unquestionably Clover Hill who died in October 1997 after two decades at stud has succeeded King of Diamonds as Ireland's premier sire of jumpers. There are indeed influential voices in the Irish breeding industry who say that Clover Hill is by far the more outstanding sire. This, however, has yet to be proved.

Both Clover Hill and King of Diamonds have in common the fact that both were Irish Draughts with thoroughbred behind them. Clover Hill was nearer to the General Studbook than his rival since his sire was Golden Beaker, a thoroughbred racehorse. The King of Diamonds thoroughbred links were further away. Without this thoroughbred influence, however, there can be little doubt that neither of these famous Irish stallions would, have achieved the prominence which they have gained as sires of jumpers.

Clover Hill in terms of pedigree was a halfbred horse. He was included in the Irish Draught stallion list because he had good Irish Draught pedigree on his dam side and was perceived to be the type of horse which could produce progeny which could be registered without reproach in the Irish Draught Studbook. At that time inspection was carried out by a specialist Department of Agriculture vet, in this case Dick Jennings, and the studbook was still open, with the role of thoroughbred blood as an improver recognised and accepted by the authorities.

Clover Hill spent all his stud life with Philip Heenan in Co Tipperary. He was bred, however, in Co Galway, by Stan Page out of a grey Irish Draught mare by Tara called Ohilly Beauty. There is no registered record of the second dam but she is said to be a black mare by Clareman (429).

Unlike King of Diamonds, Clover Hill never went out on the showjumping track. He was short listed to make a sire as a two year old by Dick Jennings, the Department of Agriculture inspector whose duty it was to select and place stallions around the country. How Clover Hill got to Philip Heenan is a story in its own right. Bord an gCapall which was the industry's appointed authority in those days had started a drive to boost exports and was staging special sales at Gowran Park racecourse. They brought in a Moroccan purchasing commission who wanted to bring stallions back with them. Heenan had stallions for sale and Jennings promised to replace them. He brought on two thoroughbreds to Ringroe Stud but Heenan wanted an Irish Draught for lighter mares as well.

Clover Hill went to Ringroe late in his second year. He went on the Register in 1976 and from the outset his progeny offered breeders a jump. Like every other unknown stallion getting him started was not easy and business for a time was slow. But when he died in 1997 Clover Hill had 1730 foals registered.

Philip Heenan

Philip Heenan had his own approach to his business. He exasperated rival stallion owners by only charging £10 for service. Even twenty years on his fees were only £30. There was, of course, an innate shrewdness in his approach. Heenan had good stallions. He was very much his own man and he knew that cheaper rates plus a growing reputation for performance would bring him the volume of mares that was needed to make his horses a success.

This is surely a magic man. Birds fly down from the skies to alight on his shoulders and peck corn from his hands. Fish float sublimely in his water trough. Stallions and visiting mare owners are under total control. A breeder might arrive seeking a service from a particular sire and leave having been told to put his mare under a different horse entirely.

Although Heenan's reputation for eccentricity spread countrywide so too did the reputations of his horses. Incredibly as the years went by he notched up scores for having the most popular sires in the country, covering 100 mares or more each season with individual sires, and equally incredibly it seemed that they were producing an outstanding complement of jumpers. The secret, of course, lay in the numbers of mares that were travelling to Ringroe. Numbers were the name of the game. For their part breeders realised that not just were the Heenan stallions cheaper than anybody else's, if the mares that were brought to them were good enough, they would deliver the goods.

The fact that Heenan's stallions were considerably cheaper than anyone else's would have counted for little in the fullness of time had not they been able to produce jumpers. However, it has to be said that there was a fair proportion of mare owners who made the journey to Ringroe purely on the basis that they were getting a bargain.

Visiting the Heenan stud in the days when Clover Hill was alive was an experience. There was always a queue, horseboxes in the carpark, mare owners sitting patiently on a bench in the yard or standing around prepared to give a hand to hold whichever mare was next on the list for whatever sire that Heenan produced. Some of them did not in fact often get the sire of their choice. Heenan would make a snap judgement himself on whatever stallion suited a particular mare and you could take it or leave it. Heenan likes an audience and is quite prepared to play to the gallery. He has all the trappings of a good showman, with his birds which are trained to fly down and sit on his shoulders or on his cap, taking pieces of bread or grain from his hand, and tickling fish which float in the water tank. Jack Russell terriers provide an additional animal ambience.

The leading out of the stallion to the mare at Ringroe is a show in itself. There are always willing hands to hobble and twitch the mares which are brought up to a strongly fenced arena just above the stables. The stallion master leads out his horse which marches obediently behind him. There is no fuss, no excitement, the stallion master waits until the horse is ready, the horse waits for the word of command.

Quiet, easy going, dressed in a countryman's working clothes and cap, Heenan always leads out the stallions himself, although he has had helpers in the last few years. He has the countryman's unhurried regulatory use of time. No matter how many people are waiting in the yard, he will close down at lunch time and go off. There is no rushing of stallions into covering. If a horse has had a mare he will be made to wait until he is really ready before he gets the next.

Impressive Performers

One of the most remarkable aspects of Philip Heenan's stallion operation is not so much that he had Clover Hill, but that he also stood some of the most impressive performers on the

Irish stallion scene over nearly three decades. Ballinvella is a case in point. This horse too produced progeny with mighty jumps and contributed his share of top class international performers, of which the best known is perhaps Bowriver Queen. There were other important sires at Ringroe over the years including Light Brigade, Smooth Stepper, Delamain and Leabeg.

Tara

The Irish Draught sire Tara (369) has had an important influence on contemporary performance. Two separate positions take him into the record books. His contribution as the sire of the dam of Clover Hill is matched as the maternal grandsire of Cruising, the highest ranked Irish international jumper of 1997. Tara stood with John Blake, Scarriff, County Clare. The Blakes had a long tradition of stallion owning. Tara is remembered as a horse with a good temperament.

Tara a grey foaled in 1943 was a son of Forest Hero (298) a chesnut son of Clonmult (91) His dam was Union Hall (1697) a daughter of Woodranger (24). Tara was the sire of several stallions including Thomond (469) Ardoon (487), Atlantic Boy (527), Loop Head (540) Clonmore Boy (576), and Capall Ruadh (594). He appears as the sire of Ardoon (487) in the dam pedigree of the successful stallion **Carrabawn View** a successful sire of jumpers who bred 466 foals. Carrabawn View's sire was Glen Star (478) a son of Glenmore (448) who goes back to Kildare (40) and Young JP (12). His dam Seaview Lass (10110) is a daughter of Colman (612) by Kilcolman (538) a grandson of Tara and has the thoroughbred Cheyne on her dam side. He stands with Albert Reid, at Shinrone, Co Offaly and was bred by Sebastian King. In 2000 Carrabawn View produced the Dublin Horse Show Performance champion, Siobhan's Choice, owned by William Anderson, Newtownards, Co Down.

Carrabawn View has a 1989 stallion son **Dunkerrin Grey Mist** (809) bred from the Prefairy (TB) mare Boston Burglar, the mare that produced Pride of Shaunlara. He stands with Deirdre and Donal Feely in Roscommon who bought him from Tony Beegan of Ballinasloe in 2000. Dunkerrin Grey Mist was approved in 1993 and was top scorer of the performance testing that year. His thoroughbred backbreeding is reflected by his athleticism. He stands 163 cms and has 24cms of bone. The Feeleys have a number of stallions but this is their first and only Irish Draught. Dunkerrin Grey Mist was bred by John Hoolan in Offaly.

The showring succcesses of two of his progeny, both owned by Pat and Elizabeth Reaney, attracted the attention of breeders. In 2000, a colt foal out of Miss R, a Quality Brood Mare by Clontoo Lad was top foal at the national Irish Draught Show. In 2001 a filly foal from the same dam was the champion foal at the show. She later made £2,400 at the Irish Draught National sale at Cavan. Dunkerrin Grey Mist has 99 foals.

In 2001 the Irish Horse Board approved another son of Carrabawn View to stand as a stallion. This is Come T (870) a daughter of the O'Malley (713) mare Orla (108780) out of Terence Lady (8861). O'Malley was by Slievenamon and stood with Nicholas Allen, Rostrevor Co Down. Terence Lady foaled 1971 was a daughter of Terence. Come T was bred by Mary Frances Doherty and is owned by Nicholas Brannifff, Downpatrick Co. Down.

The **Woodranger** influence in the Tara dam pedigree represents an old and highly successful line which produced a number of excellent broodmares including Enniskeane Countess, the dam of Kildalton Countess who went from Billy Cotter in Cork to Kildalton Agricultural College in 1973 and bred several stallion sons including Diamond Lad (695) one of the higher rated Irish Draught performance sires of the eighties and nineties.

Woodranger (24) a grey born in 1898 was bred from a Liberator (TB) mare and entered in the first Irish Draught Horse Studbook published by the Department of Agriculture in 1918. The line in Ireland has survived only in mares, but in the 1997 edition of the *Irish Draught Horse Yearbook*, Robin and Margaret Cook who ran the Roma Irish Draught Stud in Devon told their personal story of how they rescued the last of the stallion line, Timahoe Heather, who had been bred in England from an old but successful mare called April Morn. They tracked down Timahoe Heather at the age of twenty and although he only survived for one covering season they got nineteen out of twenty one mares in foal to him. Two colts were approved as stallions by the Irish Draught Horse Society GB.

Seacrest (728) foaled in 1979 was a son of **Knockboy** (700) a jumping sire by The Kerryman (492) out of a mare by Tara called Seaspray (6550) This mare also bred a stallion son of King of Diamonds, Kintara (696).

Seacrest, a Grade A jumping stallion was the sire which covered the Irish army's international jumping mare Mullacrew to produce **Cruising**. The success of Cruising as a top class showjumper is unquestionably a marker for the concept of purpose breeding from proven jumping lines. While performance testing is very much the buzz word of the new century and beyond and the watchword of the new Horse Board

Co-op, credit must be given to Bord na gCapall for its pioneering work with Flagmount Boy and other stallions and for the union of Seacrest and Mullacrew.

Both Seacrest and Cruising are based with Mary McCann at Hartwell Stud in County Kildare. Cruising has become a proven sire of jumpers in his own right. Breeders are supporting him and his foals have been making extremely good prices. He has some promising performers out on the national and international tracks. It is significant for the Irish Draught as a breed, however, that Tara appears in the dam pedigrees of the two most important stallions of the eighties and nineties, Clover Hill and Cruising. The first is in the record books because of the contribution he has made through his progeny. The second is in the record books because in difficult times he became the mainstay of the Irish international jumping team and at the end of 1997 rose to fifth position in the World showjumping rankings.

It seems that **Clareman** (429) a chesnut foaled in 1948 by Merville Prince (309) by Black Comet (52) going back to Comet No 1 in the Irish Draught Stud Book is in the Clover Hill dam line. If so this is also important pedigree. Clareman was a successful producer of mares and of course represented an influential line of old time breeding.

Golden Beaker

Golden Beaker, the sire of Clover Hill, was an Approved thoroughbred stallion who stood with Michael Moran, Kylegan, Kylebrack, Loughrea, Co Galway. A chesnut foaled in 1965 he was by Arctic Storm by Arctic Star out of Corbally Princess by Preciptic. He was a smallish horse measured for the Register at sixteen hands with eight inches of bone. He died in 1978.

The distinguished and long serving Irish racing correspondent Tony Power in a letter to the *Irish Field* in January 2001 said: "It is no surprise that Clover Hill was a success. His sire Golden Beaker and Golden Beaker's dam Corbally Princess were both tough old battlers that won their share of races and Golden Beaker kept winning over three seasons as a sound, honest horse.

"He should be, as his sire Arctic Storm, which was trained by John Oxx of Sinndar fame, won the Irish 2,000 guineas and Newmarket Champion Stakes, as well as being beaten by a short head in the Irish Derby and a length in the King George and Queen Elizabeth Stakes at Ascot behind Match and Aurelius.

"Clover Hill's sire line produced courageous, sound horses; horses that could race and could be taught to jump."

Coille Mor Hill

Clover Hill's most distinguished Irish Draught stallion son is Coille Mor Hill (840) brown 1987 ex Lawrencetown Lassy by One Wing (TB). He is owned by Michael McKeigue, Craughwell, Lawrencetown, Ballinasloe, Co Galway. This Grade A and international showjumping stallion ridden by Tom Slattery spent his first season in the top ranks in 1997 and won the VHI £2000 Grand Prix at Cavan in October. He won three Grand Prix in 1996, Cavan Indoor and Enniskerry and Callaighstown and by 2001 had 30 Grand Prix wins to his credit. He was approved in 1996. At the 2000 registration he had 135 foals registered.

Coille Mor Hill is the breed's flagship at the start of the twenty first century. Without him the Irish Draught would have very little impact on the jumping scene. He is an exceptional Grand Prix performer and has a special message to breeders in terms of pedigree. There is thoroughbred close behind in sire and dam. Clover Hill brings Golden Beaker, and Lawrencetown Lassy has One Wing a son of The Phoenix. Thoroughbred blood has brought performance to the Irish Draught. It is the only source and if the breed is to blossom as a performance breed in the years ahead, special attention will have to be given to those bloodlines which carry Thoroughbred and also and perhaps more importantly to bring in outside blood once more.

The breed will be nothing if it cannot produce top class jumpers and what cannot be found in the studbook must be brought in from outside. A possible way foward which might offer some solace to the purists is to look at the important entire sport horse performers. Coolcorron Cool Diamond by Glidawn Diamond offers a rich pedigree with King of Diamonds and Ben Purple in the sire line and the thoroughbred back breeding on both sides of the dam, Shining Crown and Cassanant. Boherdeal Clover offers Clover Hill and three dashes of thoroughbred in the backbreeding of his dam Virginia Wolfa, Right Royal, Italian Girl and Zolferine.

Cooper's Hill

Coopers Hill (844) bay 1990 ex Corlisheen Beauty (10375) by Mountain View (638) out of the Lahinch sport horse mare Corker Del is owned by John A Cogan, Corlisheen Riverstown, Co Sligo and stands with Sandra Stuart, Enniskillen Rd, Sligo. This horse was Approved in October 1997 following performance testing and at the 2000 registration had 113 foals. Coopers Hill and Finns Clover Inn (see below) share the same dam pedigree. Corlisheen Beauty bred the dam of Finns Clover Inn, Thunder Girl.

There are important influences on both sides of this dam

pedigree. Lahinch appears as the sire of the second dam Corker Del (ISH) while on the maternal side, Corker Grey goes back through Milestone to Galty Boy, a recognised sire of jumpers. Lahinch (558) was a son of Laughton 2 out of a Mount Leinster mare and produced ten stallion sons. He stood with Vincent Faughnan in Co Leitrim. Milestone (498), the sire of Corker Grey and grandson of Galty Boy was an influential sire in his own right. Milestone had eleven stallion sons. He stood with Tom Hodgins in Kilkenny and for a time with Timothy Sullivan in Laois. His dam was Doree Maid by the halfbred Royal Gem. His leading contributions to the stallion Register were Pride of Shaunlara and Legaun Prince

Diamond Clover

Diamond Clover ex Highlight Girl is owned by Wilfred Atkinson, Capponellan Stud, Durrow, Co Laois. This 1990 chesnut is a daughter of the King of Diamonds mare Highlight Girl (RID 10693) out of the AID mare Highlight. Diamond Clover was approved in 1993 and at the 2000 registration had 234 foals recorded.

Highlight has interesting connections in her backbreeding. Her maternal grandam, Laughton's Belle was a daughter of Bell Laughton (578) by Laughton's Last out of Inishowen (399). Laughton's Last was a famous hunting stallion ridden by Ikey Bell when he hunted in England. Laughton's Last was out of a mare by the thoroughbred Royal Tip and was bred by the Hodgins family in Co Kilkenny. He was the son of the first Laughton, a thoroughbred horse by Castlereagh out of a William the Conqueror mare. Laughton's Last produced a second Laughton (446) out of a Kings Herald (TB) mare. He was registered as an Irish Draught stallion. Laughton 2 became an important sire who had stallion sons and a series of stallion descendants through Lahinch (558). Laughton's Last went back to the Hodgins farm and stood there for several years from 1937. See section on Laughton later.

Inishowen went back to **Galty Boy** (97) on her sire side. Galty Boy was a grandson of Young JP number 12 in Horse Studbook and a foundation sire with enormous influence on the breed. Galty Boy produced seven stallion sons. One of his competition produce was the famous Irish Army jumper Limerick Lace. Seamus Hayes had another exceptional jumper by him, Snowstorm. He became a recognised sire of jumpers. One of his descendants was Errigal by Silvermines, a son of Galty Boy. Errigal was the sire of King of Diamonds, the most influential Irish jumping sire ever.

Finns Clover Inn

Finns Clover Inn (850) ex Thunder Girl (11151) by Diamond Lad, a 1995 bay is owned by Patrick Finn, Aughrim, Ballinasloe Co Galway. Thunder Girl's dam was Corlisheen Beauty by Mountain View (638) out of the ISH mare Corker Dell. Finns Clover Inn was approved in 1998 following central performance testing. He was bred by Padraig Clarke. Thunder Girl also carried Galty Boy on her dam side.

Golden Trump

Golden Trump (799) by Diamonds are Trumps is a grandson of Clover Hill on his dam side. She was Silver Hills out of the Silverstone Mare, Jalna. Golden Trump is discussed in the Chapter on King of Diamonds.

Philip Clover

Philip Clover (855) ex Ballyadam Beauty (10728) by Ben Purple (580) a 1993 grey is owned by Geoffrey Curran, Ballyadam, Fenor, Co Waterford. He was bred by his owner. He was Approved in 1999, He has been show jumped and qualified for the RDS national classes for the three years from 1997. He was placed second twice at the RDS in 1999. He was ridden by Geoffrey Curran Jr from 1997 to 1999 but in 2000 the ride was taken by Francis Connors as Geoffrey had gone to the Army Equitation School. Ballyadam Beauty's dam was Dawn Beauty 2 by Nordlys, Ballyadam Beauty has bred a number of foals which have been exported to Europe as showjumpers and event horses.

The Pride of Gloster

The Pride of Gloster (842) dark dapple bay 1993 out of the Pride of Shaunlara mare Bantry's Pride (10791) a daughter of the Bantry Pearl mare Lough Glynne (10308) is owned by Sheila Hough, Main Street, Banagher, Co Offaly. He was Approved in October 1997 after performance testing. At the 1999 registration he had 6 foals recorded. Lough Glynne was the dam of the stallion Kildalton Son. Bantry's Pride bred three foals altogether by Clover Hill and two by Clover's Dream. She had nine foals in total up to 2000.

The Pride of Gloster won the Irish Draught colt foal class in the RDS in 1993. He qualified in 1996 for the Bank of Ireland Young Irelander. Tom Slattery rode him for the 1997 open competition performance test. His first foals were on the ground in 1999 and an Irish Draught colt foal was second in his class in the RDS and went on to become reserve champion foal. The same foal was second in the Irish Draught National Show and was first at Ballinasloe in 1999. The dam of this foal, Slyguff's Dream (10792) is the dam of the stallion Clover's Dream who stands with Philip Heenan.

Mackney Clover

In 2001 the Irish Horse Board approved Mackney Clover

(867) as a registered stallion. A 1996 chesnut he is out of Thunder Girl (11151) by Diamond Lad (695). His pedigree brings together the two outstanding jumping lines in Irish Draught performance. He was bred and is owned by Padraig Clarke, Balinasloe, Co Galway. Thunder Girl bred the stallion Finn's Clover Inn.

Some International Showjumpers by Clover Hill

Ballaseyer Twilight

Ballaseyr Twilight formerly Sure Coin, 1989 bay gelding by Clover Hill out of Ballynagran Natalie (ISH) by Prince Riza (TB) bred by Betty Parker, Dunganstown, Wicklow, owned by Ballaseyr Stables. Ridden by Cameron Hanley he represented Ireland in four Nations Cups at Helsinki, Falsterbo, Hickstead and Rome in 2000. He also won the Kings Cup at Hickstead CSIO and the Kerrygold Grand Prix at Dublin.

Boherdeal Clover

Boherdeal Clover 1991 ISH stallion (RID) out of Virginia Wolfa (ISH) by Regular Guy (TB) bred by Pamela Miller, Mount Cashel Stud, Roscommon. Owned by Padraig Goonan, Crinkle, Birr, Co Offaly. Leased to Irish Army. Rider Lt David O'Brien. Won Grand Prix at Cavan 2000. He was on winning Nations Cup team at Falsterbo, Sweden in 2001.

Cagney

Cagney 1980 Bay gelding won the $50,000 Cuddy International Grand Prix in 1996 at London Ontario Canada in 1996 ridden by Eric Lamaze, Canada. In 1997 he won $50,000 Volvo qualifier at Bromont, $25,000 Sunfeest Grand Prix Palgrave Ontario and was second in three other Canadian Grand Prix. In 2000 won the $175,000 Chrysler Classic Derby, Spruce Meadows

Carling King

Carling King 1991 chesnut gelding by Clover Hill out of Gortnagger Star (ISH) by Chairlift (TB) bred by Dr Past Geraghty, Glenamaddy, Co. Galway, owned by Sally Glassman, USA. Ridden by Kevin Babington he represented Ireland in five Nations Cups at Aachen, Rotterdam, Calgary, Hickstead and

Rome in 2000. He was also third in the $50,000 Spillers Eminole Feed Grand Prix in Ocala, Florida. In 1999 he was fourth in the $40,000 Grand Prix at Pittsburgh. In 2000 on winning Nations Cups teams at Hickstead, Calgary and Rotterdam.

Clover Flush

Clover Flush 1991 stallion ISH out of the Queen of Trumps (AID) by King of Diamonds (RID). Bred by Carmel Ryan, Waterford. Produced in Ireland by Jack Doyle. Won World Cup Qualifier 2000 at Victoria, Aus. Rider: Greg Smith

Clover Choice

Clover Choice won Cairo Grand Prix 1996 ridden by James Kernan

Clover Heights

Clover Heights 1988 gelding out of Craigue Beauty (ISH) by Smooth Stepper (TB) bred by Fintan Flannelly, Kill, Co Kildare. Rider: Dick Carvin USA. In 2000 won $25,000 Ariat Grand Prix, Idaho.

Clover Leaf

1984 mare bred by Liam O'Meara, Feigh East, Borrisokane, Co Tipperary, out of Feigh Lass (ISH) by Merlin (TB) Owned by Danielle Montelone. Second in $25,000 Grand Prix at North Salem, New York, May 1998, won $50,000 World Cup qualifier at Blianville, July 1998 ridden by Leslie Howard USA In 2000 won at Tampa and Toronto. On USA Nations Cup winning team at Toronto

Coille Mor Hill

Coille Mor Hill 1897 stallion out of Lawrencetown Lassy (RID) by One Wing (TB) bred and owned by Michael McCaigue,

Lawrencetown, Ballinasloe, Co Galway. Rider: Tom Slattery. Winner of 30 Grand Prix In 2000 won GP at Clonshire

Convent Hill Diamond

Convent Hill Diamond 1988 gelding bred by M.Kenna, Ferbane, Co Offaly out of a King of Diamonds mare. Won Hickstead Speed grand prix in 1996 ridden by Robert Splaine.

Dreampoint Clover

Dreampoint Clover (ISH) 1991 bay gelding by Clover Hill out of Gurtray Colleen (ISH) by Middle Temple (TB) bred by Count Eoin P. O'Kelly, Co. Galway, owned by Miss M O'Brien, O'Brien Office Systems, Cork. Ridden by Denis Coakley he represented Ireland in the Nations Cup at Linz in 2000. He also won the Grand Prix at Linz and the Grand Prix and the Masters at Millstreet.

Flo Jo

Flo Jo a 1984 grey mare by Clover Hill out of a King of Diamonds mare Twinkle was bred by the late Seamus Hughes at Cuffesgrange, Co Kilkenny and is ridden by Marion Hughes. She won the Queen's Cup in 1995 and retained it in 1996. Flo Jo won the Grand Prix in Vejer de La Frontera, Spain in 1997 and the Kerrygold Speed Championship at Dublin. On winning Irish Nations Cup team Zagreb 1997. In 2000 she won the Grand Prix at Portimao. An outstanding performance mare.

Frisky IV

Frisky IV (ex Ringwood Skyhigh) 1990 gelding out of Fiddlers Field (TB) by Skyliner (TB) Bred by TR Horgan, Cluggin House, Oola, Co Limerick Rider: Ms Dehlia Oeuvray SUI

Gelvin Clover

Gelvin Clover is a 1993 son of Clover Hill out of Culdearg

(11146) by Ginger Dick (643) out of an AID mare Golden Fox by Stone Fox (TB) He was bred by Kieran Rowley, Culmore, Swinford, Co Mayo. Gelvin Clover won the Irish Horse Board's seven year old championship in 2000 and represented the studbook at Lanaken. He won the Mini Grand Prix at Dublin Horse Show 2001 ridden by Clem McMahon. Gelvin Clover is owned by Robert and May Scott from Co Derry.

Killaloe Clover

Jumping for Austrian Nations Cup team placed third at Zagreb 1997 ridden by Ulrich Domaingo

Killone Abbey

Killone Abbey 1988 chesnut gelding bred by P. Normoyle, Ennis, Co Clare out of a Jab (TB) mare. Won the Derby at Falsterbo and was third in the Pulsar International at Spruce Meadows, ridden by Commdt Gerry Mullins who retired from competition and was promoted to command of the Army Equitation School.

Rincoola Abu

Rincoola Abu 1991 bay mare by Cruising out of Holly Hill (ISH) by Clover Hill bred by Harold McGahern, Rincoola, Granard, Co Longford. Ridden by Capt Gerry Flynn she represented Ireland in three nations Cups at Athens, Helsinki and Falsterbo in 2000. She also won the Grand Prix at Helsinki CSIO and was second in the Derby at Berlin CSI-A. In 1999 she won the Grand Prix at Tripoli CSI-A and the Young Horse Championship at Wiesbaden. In 2000 she won the Grand Prix at Helsinki

Tell the Difference

Tell the Difference 1989 mare by Clover Hill out of Raheen (ISH) by Nordlys (TB) bred by Ms Catherine Kenny,

Deerpark, Moyistown, Belmont, Co Offaly. Ridden by P Freimuller, Switzerland

Uptons LB

Uptons LB 1986 bay gelding was foaled in 1986 out of a 15.2 hh Welsh cross mare Upton's Prunelle. His breeder Mrs Leo McKenna said that he was the most common foal with the worst conformation she had ever seen. He was tried over a pole at three and his performance compensated his owner for his unpromising appearance. Uptons LB was broken in by the McKenna's daughter Cheryl at four years of age. He was easy to do and kind in every way. By then he was 17 hands. He went to Mennell Watson for a few shows and was then laid off as it was obvious that he needed more time to mature.

In 1994 he qualified for the Horse of the Year Show in three classes, the Newcomers and Foxhunters and the Olympic Talent Spotters. He won the Newcomers, was fourth in the Foxhunters and went on to finish third in the Olympic Talent Spotters.

In 1995 he competed in his first season as a Grade A, competed at Hickstead and the following year was in the international classes at Wembley. He jumped at Millstreet in the Volvo World Cup and Irish Derby and then headed for Olympia. He was put on Britain's Nations Cup team at the end of the year in Belgium and finished fourth in the Grand Prix. Britain finished second in the Nations Cup, Upton took the award for the most consistent horse at the show and did his own lap of honour. It was an emotional moment for his owner/breeder and she greeted it, she says, with tears streaming down her face and heart exploding

Pride of Shaunlara

Pride of Shaunlara stood at Suma Stud in Co Meath run by Susan Lanigan O'Keeffe and Marily Power. Suma pioneered quality standards in the modern Irish Draught and became one of the most successful enterprises in Irish Draught breeding. Pride of Shaunlara had seventeen stallion sons and was the sire and grandsire of countless showring performers. He produced jumpers and eventers as well but would not rate as highly in this sphere as either King of Diamonds or Clover Hill.

The grey Pride of Shaunlara was foaled in 1979, a son of Milestone (498) out of the Prefairy (TB) mare Boston Burglar. He stood 16.2 hh and had nine and a half inches of bone. He established a reputation as a performance sire and a producer of stallion sons. He has 364 registered progeny. His stallion sons stood in Ireland and England. In 2001 he still had four stallions on the Irish register. Pride of Shaunlara mares have been good producers. His daughter Tara Sky is the dam of Crosstown Dancer.

In 2000 Suma stud turned to Continentals in their search for performance although they still stood Crosstown Dancer and Huntingfield Rebel, a winner of the Irish Draught class at Dublin and son of Glenagyle Rebel, the stud's Grade A showjumper which was exported to Zimbabwe. His dam was the successful Blue Peter mare Whippy. Suma's preference would have been for a thoroughbred stallion but successful thoroughbred producers of showjumpers are now hard to find. They hit on a four year Dutch bred horse VDL Arkansas and succeeded in winning the four year old jumping championship at Dublin Horse Show. Suma Stud had taken a new road to excellence.

There will probably always be Irish Draughts at this County Meath breeding centre. Their successes over the years were remarkable. Championship after championship fell to Suma progeny and the stud set a very clear headline for other breeders. Quality which had been missing for some time was restored to the Irish Draught.

Other breeders followed their example. Other countries purchased their stallions. It seems clear, however, that Suma has recognised that at present there are limits to what the Irish Draught can achieve as a performance horse. The struggle between the Irish Draught and the Continental is an unequal contest. There may be a great deal of truth in the often expressed view that the Irish Draught can get to Grade A but not much further.

Milestone sire of Pride of Shaunlara, foaled in 1957, produced eleven stallion sons. He stood with Tom Hodgins in Kilkenny and for a time with Timothy Sullivan in Laois. His dam was Doree Maid by the thoroughbred Royal Gem and his leading contributions to the stallion register were Pride of Shaunlara and Legaun Prince, while Lisheen, Silverstone and Huntsman had more limited reputations. Roll On had a reputation as a performance sire in his own right registering over 200 foals.

Pride of Toames

Pride of Shaunlara's contribution to the stallion register includes Pride of Toames out of the Glen Lad (458) mare Toames Beauty (7260) the sire of Grey Macha and Prospect

Pride. Pride of Toames was a successful sire and left 470 registered progeny behind him including two stallion sons. One of these **Grey Macha** out of the Aughadown mare Ballybane Grace has over 400 registered foals. Grey Macha has two sons currently on the stallion register, Agherlow and Mourne Mountain Star, while Prospect Pride has been equally successful with over 450 foals. He sired **Grange Bouncer**, who has been making strides as an eventer. Pride of Shaunlara has still four sons on the register, the veteran Prospect Pride, Parkmore Pride, Suma's Murphy's Law and Townrath Pride.

Amongst his other deceased stallion sons are King Elvis, a full brother to Toames Beauty, and Silver Hunter. Silver Hunter out of the sport horse mare Inchigeela Lass by the thoroughbred Keepatwoatwo has produced the stallion Fast Silver out of the champion mare Fast Woman by Slievenamon, and the black stallion Springpark Jack the Lad. King Elvis left over 100 foals including Annaghdown Star.

Agherlow

Agherlow (810) is a 1988 grey son of Grey Macha out of the Dickie (577) mare Sligo Star (10146). Her dam Carrowilkeen Marigold was a daughter of Boherbue (544). He was bred by Michael Burke and stands with Gladys Nesbitt, Drumhowan Stud, Co Monaghan. He has 57 registered foals.

Annaghdown Star

Annaghdown Star is a grandson of Pride of Shaunlara by King Elvis (708) out of a Glenside (563) mare Annaghdown Gold (10439) a daughter of Annaghdown Rose by Blackwater Lad. He was foaled in 1987 and bred by Martin Conneely. He stands with Roy Butler Crumlin, Co Antrim. He was previously with Paddy Kelly, Ravensdale, Dundalk who had him for the high points of his career. A grey he measures 17 hands. He has won the Irish Draught stallion class at Dublin Horse Show on three occasions and been reserve twice. He has produced showjumpers. Annaghdown Star has made his own contribution to the stallion register with Star Kingdom out of the King of Diamonds mare Ireland's Diamond. He has 144 registered foals.

Fast Silver

Fast Silver (829) was foaled in 1991 and was bred by Sean Walshe who stood his sire Silver Hunter (681). He is owned by Elizabeth Deane, Buttevant, Co Cork and stands with PJ McCarthy, at Bandon. His dam was the show mare Fast Woman (10289) by Slievenamon (682) Her dam was the Kantogher Pride mare Hard and Fast (6254). He has 40 registered foals.

Grange Bouncer

Grange Bouncer (848) is a grandson of Pride of Shaunlara by Prospect Pride (738). His dam is the Kilmore Heather (608) mare Grange Heather (10331) out of the Tara mare Casting Vote. Grange Heather also bred two showjumpers Grange Power and Grange Fields and an eventer Hemisphere. She is a full sister to Paddy's Pride sire of advanced eventer Triton Brigadier in England. A grey, foaled in 1992, Grange Bouncer was bred by Jack Lambert and is owned by Ann Lambert, Killinick, Co Wexford. Grange Bouncer is proving a successful eventer in his own right and has produced successful progeny, including Beal na Blath winner of the Four year old Young Event Horse final and overall championship at Millstreet 2000. He is also the sire of eventer Grange Harbour.

In 2001 Grange Bouncer was 10 pts short of Grade B under SJAI rules. He won Statoil, Gain and Boomerang qualifiers and was second in the Young Riders Showjumping final at Dublin Horse Show 1997. He was an intermediate eventer from his first season and won three novice one day events in 2000, finished seventh in Blarney Three Day event 2000 and won the seven year old upwards division at the Future event horse league at Naas 2001. Grange Harbour won the four year old section at this fixture.

Grey Macha

Grey Macha was a 1981 grey grandson of Pride of Shaunlara by Pride of Toames out of the show mare Ballybane Grace (7846) by Aughadown (565) There is no other recorded pedigree on the dam side. Standing 17 hands, Grey Macha was bred and was owned by Bernard Stanford of Gort, Co Galway. He has been a successful sire and has 409 registered foals. He has a sport horse stallion son Grey Tyrera. He bred the stallion Gort Boy standing in England, Mourne Mountain Star (806) and Agherlow (810). Macha Breeze stands in USA.

Grey Macha's long and fruitful career resulted in the production of some quality stock. At Dublin Horse Show in 2001 three Grey Macha mares figured in the prize list for one of the Irish Draught mare classes. He died in 2001

Mourne Mountain Star

Mourne Mountain Star (806) is a 1988 son of Grey Macha out of the Rathlin Star (707) mare Bay Queen (10551). Her dam was Carranrod Lass an AID mare by Uisneagh Hill (514). He was bred by James Connolly and stands with Owen J Duffy, Shercock, Co Monaghan. He has 63 registered foals.

Parkmore Pride

Parkmore Pride a grey foaled in 1991 is out of an Atlantic Boy (527) mare Parkmore Jewel. Atlantic Boy is a son of Tara (369) who appears in the pedigree of Clover Hill and Cruising as already discussed. Parkmore Jewel's dam Derryfrench Rose is a daughter of Laughton (446). Parkmore Pride was bred by Patrick Wafer of Carnew, Co Wicklow. Parkmore Jewel was a well known mare which showjumped and bred a number of foals. Parkmore Pride was her fifth. He stands with Fleur Bryan, Portarlington.

Prospect Pride

Prospect Pride (738) was foaled in 1980. A grey he was bred from a Glen Star (478) mare Mermaid 3 which had no dam line pedigree recorded. He stands with Patrick Leacy, Enniscorthy, Co Wexford. He was bred by Michael Aherne. He has 453 registered foals.

Springpark Jack the Lad

Springpark Jack the Lad (802) is a 1988 black grandson of Pride of Shaunlara by Silver Hunter out of the thoroughbred Tiverton's Pride mare Knock Dana (8358). There is no other pedigree recorded on the dam side. He was bred by Seamus Carey and is owned by Jean Steenson, Ballybay, Co Monaghan. He has 45 registered foals.

Star Kingdom

Star Kingdom (856) is a grey 1994 great grandson of Pride of Shaunlara by Annaghdown Star. His dam was Ireland's Diamond (10008) by King of Diamonds out of Tullagh Ireland's Glory by Merrion (447). He was bred and is owned by Timothy Carey, Tullaghansleek Stud, Co Westmeath. He was Approved in 1999 following central performance testing. He has ten registered foals.

Suma's Murphy's Law

Suma's Murphy's Law (803) foaled in 1988 was bred from a Skylark (627) mare Softee (10243) Her dam Goodness Gracious 2 (7933) was by the thoroughbred Cheyne. He was bred by Susan Lanigan O'Keeffe and regularly hunted. He stands at Suma Stud. He has 78 registered foals.

Townrath Pride

Townrath Pride (771) was foaled in 1984 and bred by James Norris. His dam was a Skylark mare Townrath Rose (10812). He stands with James Dunne, Catholes, Ballyfin, Co Laois. He has 222 registered foals.

Female Line

Pride of Shaunlara mares have been good producers. His stock did exceptionally well both in the showring and showjumping. His daughter Tara Sky is the dam of Crosstown Dancer who himself has a young stallion son the 1996 Crosstown Pride. Another Pride of Shaunlara mare produced Blue Henry, the sire of current stallion Crannagh Hero and another daughter produced the dam of the son of Ben Purple, The Bard. This was Suma's Blue Heaven by Blue Peter. Pride of Toames produced Brehans Pride (10979) the dam of the Kildalton Gold stallion Herrero. The dam of Clover Hill's The Pride of Gloster is Bantry's Pride by Pride of Shaunlara.The paternal grand dam of Blue Champion by Blue Henry is Knockavaher Pride.

Blue Champion

Blue Champion a 1986 grey by Blue Henry (744), a son of Blue Peter (536) carries Pride of Shaunlara as the sire of his sire's dam Knockavaher Pride (10292) His dam was Belgrove Beauty (10361) a daughter of Sir Henry 11 (614) by Poulgorm (546). The grandam was Murrough Beauty (8098) a daughter of Laughton (446). Blue Champion was bred by Deirdre Lowry and stands with Patrick Scarry, Ballinasloe, Co Galway. He has 45 registered foals.

Crannagh Hero

Crannagh Hero (713) is another son of Blue Henry out of the Poulgorm mare Silver Queen (8279). Poulgorm was by Abbeylara (478). Silver Queen's dam was Glanmire Light who has no recorded pedigree. Crannagh Hero foaled 1986 was bred by Timothy Sullivan and stands with Francis Healy, Birdhill, Co Tipperary. He has 145 registered foals.

Crosstown Dancer

Crosstown Dancer (821) is discussed in the section on King of Diamonds. He is a son of Flagmount Diamond out of the Pride of Shaunlara mare Tara Sky (10499) and was bred by Fintan Branigan. He stands at Suma Stud. He has 227 registered foals.

Crosstown Pride

Crosstown Pride (851) is a 1995 son of Crosstown Dancer out of the Western Pride (704) mare Lake View Pride (757). Her dam is Garrybawn Lark (120889) by Skylark (627) He is bred and owned by Fintan Branigan and was Approved in 1998 following central performance testing. Exported.

The Pride of Gloster

The Pride of Gloster 842 is a 1993 dark dapple bay out of the Pride of Shaunlara mare Bantry's Pride. He is discussed in the chapter on Clover Hill.

Milestone Bloodlines

Milestone's other important son **Legaun Prince**, produced several important stallions including Rakish Paddy and **Skippy** who has several entire sons. Legaun Prince had 385 registered foals. Skippy out of a Final Problem mare produced registered stallions in England and Ireland. In Ireland, Silver Skip left 238 foals, Sandyhill Boy has 141 and Corrundulla Star 116. Skippy sired the dams of two current stallions,

Cream of Diamonds and Bobin.

Rakish Paddy (753) was a successful Grade A showjumper out of a Sunset Lad (419) mare Ballard Lass. He was a stallion class winner at Dublin Horse Show. He was bred and is owned by Sally Begg, Navan, Co Meath who campaigned him as a showjumper. He now stands with Susan Malee, Swinford, Co Mayo. He produced 169 registered foals.

Another Milestone stallion pedigree which is still current is the Silverstone-Glenvara-Silver Granite line. **Silver Granite** went to the United States and was brought back to stand in Kildare. He was bred by Noel Hamilton from his Young Ireland (526) mare Celtic Banner. Silver Granite is owned by Fintan Flanelly, Kill International Equestrian Centre and stands at Liam Togher Stud in Co Kildare. Silver Granite has 156 registered foals.

Ard Granpa (807) is a son of Silver Granite out of a Middle Temple (TB) mare. He was bred from a Middle Temple (TB) mare Lurga Lady and was bred and successfully campaigned by Heather Wright. He is now owned by Martin Shaughnessy, Co Galway. Ard Granpa has 99 registered foals

Lisheen, another son of Milestone out of a PInzari (TB) mare produced Western Pride who in turn bred Lakeview Pride and Western Light. **Western Light** (772) was bred from the Dove 2 mare Molly Bawn V1 He was bred by John Shorten and is owned by Helen Troughten, Ballinteggart Stud, Portadown, Co Armagh. He has 118 registered foals.

Sandyhill Boy (739) is a 1980 chesnut son of Skippy out the Colman (612) mare Sea View Lass. Bred by Sebastian King he stands with John Shorten, Askeaton, Co Limerick. He has

145 registered foals.

Silverstone (656) in 2001 was Milestone's surviving stallion son. Foaled in 1971 he was bred from a Merrion (447) mare Silver 9. He stands with Michael O'Regan, Rosscarbery, Co Cork. He has 195 registered foals.

Silver Granite, Silverstone and Grey Macha each have a registered ISH stallion son.

Galty Boy who appears in the King of Diamonds pedigree as the grandsire of Errigal was the grandsire of Milestone. He stood until he was twenty five years of age with Mick Buckley in Tipperary. One of his seven stallion sons was Galty's Son, the sire of Milestone. He has exercised a major performance influence in the Irish Daught world.

Not all Milestone's descendants have turned out to be exceptional producers of performance in their progeny. Undoubtedly Pride of Shaunlara was the most outstanding stallion son but Milestone's influence on the Irish Draught as a breed has been important and the ramifications of his contributions to modern pedigree extensive. Nearly 2000 foals carrying Milestone blood lines have been bred in the period from 1995 to 2000.

Ben Purple

Ben Purple (580) foaled in 1965 stood first with Denis Lucey, Ballingeary, Co Cork, and then with John McCarthy who sold him to Patrick Kinsella, Knockhouse, Kilmacow in Co Kilkenny. He subsequently went to England and established himself as an important sire there. A grey, he stood 16.3 hh and had nine and three quarter inches of bone. He was an influential stallion and represented an old breeding line going back to Young JP, number twelve in the Irish Draught Horse Book, and before him to Ploughboy. This stallion had six stallion sons who produced many of the mares of first registration in the Irish Draught Book.

Ben Purple was a son of Mountain Heather and grandson of Galty Boy. He had the champion stallion Kildare (40) in the female line on both sides of his pedigree. Kildare produced seventeen stallions and a son Pride of Cork who produced sixteen. Young JP is a foundation sire and exerts a major influence over a large number of living sires. He produced Brehon Law who in turn bred Galty Boy, whose grandson was Milestone. The role of Galty Boy as a performance influence in King of Diamonds has already been discussed.

There are currently (2002) five sons and three grandsons of Ben Purple on the stallion register. He has contributed to the female lines of a further eleven sires. There is plenty of performance the most outstanding example of which is the winner of the eventing individual gold medal at the Sydney Olympics in 2000, David O'Connor's Custom Made.

Custom Made, a son of the important thoroughbred sire Bassompierre was bred from an ISH Ben Purple mare, Purple Heather, by Mrs Kitty Horgan and her daughter Elizabeth O'Flynn, evented in Ireland by Aaron Mannion, and sold to America eventually bringing David O'Connor his Olympic titile.

Kildalton Countess

Ben Purple produced important mares. The best known of these is Kildalton Countess, bred at Kildalton Agricultural College under the equine project there managed by Norman Storey. Kildalton College acquired Billy Cotter's mare Enniskeane Countess in 1973 as a foundation mare for their enterprise. Kildalton Countess bred several stallion sons, the important **Diamond Lad** (695) in 1976, Diamonds are Trumps (711) in 1977, Kildalton King (714) in 1978 and **Glidawn Diamond** (754) in 1982. She was also the dam of Kildalton Gold, sire of Westmeath Lad (834) produced from the King of Diamonds mare Ireland's Diamond (1008).

In an article in the *Irish Draught Horse Yearbook 1996,* Norman Storey says that Kildalton Countess was barren only twice in twenty years. She bred her first foal in 1975, a filly by King of Diamonds. Her first three stallion sons were produced in the three years from 1976 to 1978. Then came two fillies Kildalton Rose and Kildalton June. Kildalton Rose is the dam of showjumper Convent Hill Diamond.

She produced only one foal by a thoroughbred, a filly by Hildenley, who also stood at Knockhouse Stud, in 1984. In 1985 and 1986 she produced two foals by Merrygold. These were Kildalton Gold and Kildalton Merrygirl. Merrygirl went on to breed the I993 Dublin Horse Show champion by the thoroughbred Skyboy. Throughout her long career she went to a diverse range of stallions including Seacrest by whom she had two colts and Prospect Pride who gave her Pride of Kildalton who won the Irish Draught National Show championship. There were two colts by Golden Warrior and her last foal in 1993 was by Suma's Murphy's Law.

In 2001 Billy Cotter relived his triumph of 1967 when he won the revived Irish Draught class at Dublin Show with Enniskeane Countess. Forty four years on a descendant mare in the Kildalton Countess dam line won the Irish Draught mare championship at Dublin Horse Show. This was Enniskeane Flash by the exported stallion Mountain Pearl. The championship marked a long and dedicated career by the Irish Draught Horse Society's life president

Ben Calverston

Ben Calverston (832) was bred by Cecilia Delaney and foaled in 1992. He stands with Susan Malee, Swinford, Co Mayo. His dam was Silver Queen, a daughter of Blue Peter (536) by Kylemore (459). No dam pedigree is recorded. He was Approved in 1994. He has 39 foals to date. Blue Peter was a performance sire. He produced Bouncer, the British international Olympics horse owned by Judy Crago. Blue Peter ended his stallion career at Suma Stud.

Holycross

Holycross (763) was foaled in 1983 and bred by William Bourke. He stood originally with Tim Sullivan of Abbeyleix and went to Timothy O'Regan of Ballygarrett Stud, near Mallow in Co Cork. His dam was June Bud by Dove 11 a son of Milestone out of Clareen Calypso. No further dam pedigree is recorded. He has 418 registered foals.

Lissarda Star

Lissarda Star (651) was foaled in 1969. The only dam pedigree recorded is his maternal sire Triumph (397) by Galtee Beg (198) a son of Galty Boy (97). He stood with Jim Buckley, Cappawhite, Co Tipperary. He had 17 registered foals.

Powerswood Purple

Powerswood Purple (737) was foaled in 1980. He was bred by Garett Phelan and stands with Martin Geoghegan, Ardrahan, Co Galway. His dam was Powerswood Best (7789) a daughter of Clareman (429). He has 518 registered foals.

The Bard

The Bard (818) was foaled in 1989 He was bred by and stands with Helen Troughton, Ballinteggart Stud, Portadown, Co Armagh. His dam was Sumas Blue Heaven, a daughter of Blue Peter out of a Pride of Shaunlara mare Knockavaher Pride. Blue Peter produced the successful Blue Rajah (536) and Blue Henry (744) sire of Blue Champion (795) and Crannagh Hero (793). He has 19 foals.

Creggan Emperor

Creggan Emperor is a son of Holycross out of an Armada Star (566) mare Carrigroe Star (9153). A chesnut he was foaled in 1989 and bred by Patrick Keena. He stands with Hugh Hennigan, Manor Stud, Castlerea, Co Roscommon. He has 100 registered foals.

Grosvenor Lad

Grosvenor Lad is a 1990 chesnut son of Holycross (763). He was foaled in 1990 and bred by PJ O'Driscoll. His dam Madam Joy is a daughter of Slyguff Hero, the full brother to King of

Diamonds, out of a mare called Carolina (6276) who was by Abbeylara. There is no further pedigree recorded on the dam side. Abbeylara traces back to Starlight and then to Comet, number one in the Irish Draught Book.

Grosvenor Lad stands with PJ O'Reilly of Louisberg, Co Mayo. He started out with John Shorten in Limerick and then stood for a year with John Murphy in Dungarvan before going to Mayo in 1995. Grosvenor Lad won the Irish Draught stallion class in Dublin in 1996. Stallions have been kept at the O'Reilly stud for over one hundred years. The family have been keen supporters of the Irish Draught starting out with Sarsfield and following up with Merry Lad. The stallion keeping tradition was established by PJ O'Reilly's grandfather Pat in 1897. Grosvenor Lad has a sport horse stallion in England, the 1997 chesnut Connaught Lad 2 owned by Dean/ McCrory, Lingfield, Surrey.

Ben Purple has exercised a strong influence through his female descendants, his most prominent daughter of course being Kildalton Countess. Unquestionably Kildalton Countess's most important stallion son was **Diamond Lad** but she produced Kildalton Gold who bred Herrero and Celtic Gold, Kildalton King, and Glidawn Diamond who bred Wyzer Diamond. Carrigbawn Coleen, another Ben Purple daughter bred Diamond King and Silver Glider; Springfield Star produced Duleek Hero; Night Nurse 2 bred Glenlara; and Ballyadam Beauty bred Philip Clover.

Diamond King

Diamond King (756) by The Conqueror is a 1983 grey grandson of King of Diamonds out of Carrigbawn Coleen (418), a daughter of Ben Purple. He is discussed in the chapter on King of Diamonds.

Donovan

Donovan (859) is a 1991 grey who carries Ben Purple as the sire of his dam Night Nurse 2 (10054). Her dam was Young Sweetheart an ISH mare by the thoroughbred Awkward Brief. Donovan is by Parnell (642) a son of Aughadown (565) by Gortlee (426). (See chapter Outcrosses)

Duleek Hero

Duleek Hero (760) is a grey 1983 grandson of King of Diamonds by Ireland's Pride (705) He is out of a daughter of Ben Purple, Springfield Star (10296). He is discussed in the chapter on King of Diamonds.

Kildalton Gold

Kildalton Gold (774) was a 1985 chesnut son of Merrygold (644) by Lahinch (558) a son of Laughton (446). His dam was Kildalton Countess (10180). He was bred by Kildalton Agricultural College and stood with Thomas Kearns, Mooncoin, Co Kilkenny. He has 553 foals. This horse was at one stage described as one of the best types of Irish Draughts in the country and became extremely popular.

Kildalton King

Kildalton King (714) is a 1978 bay son of King of Diamonds out of Kildalton Countess, a prolific brood mare and daughter of Ben Purple. He was bred by Kildalton Agricultural College and stands with Maurice Cousins, Gorey, Co Wexford. He has 435 foals. He is discussed in the chapter on King of Diamonds.

Philip Clover

Philip Clover (855) is a son of Clover Hill and is discussed in that section. .

Silver Glider

Silver Glider (770) is a 1984 grey great grandson of King of Diamonds, by The Conqueror (725) His dam was Carrigbawn Coleen (9418), a daughter of Ben Purple. He was bred by Daniel J. Crowley and stands with John McShane at Dundalk, Co Louth. He has 239 registered foals.

Welcome Diamond

Welcome Diamond (825) is a grand son of King of Diamonds by Diamond Lad (695) Diamond Lad's dam is Kildalton Countess a daughter of Ben Purple. He is discussed in the chapter on King of Diamonds

Wyzer Diamond

Wyzer Diamond (819) is a 1990 bay son of Glidawn Diamond and grandson of King of Diamonds. Glidawn Diamond is a son of Kildalton Countess a daughter of Ben Purple. He was exported to Britain and is discussed in the section Irish Draughts in Britain

Laughton

The Laughton line is an influential performance group founded by the Hodgins family. The most important descendant sire is Lahinch (558) who produced ten stallion sons. The foundation sire was Castlereagh a thoroughbred who produced the first Laughton out of a William the Conqueror (TB) mare. His son Laughton's Last out of a mare by Royal Tip (TB) produced Laughton (446) from a mare by Kings Herald (TB). Laughton (446) has twelve grandsons on the current Irish Draught stallion list.

The Hodgins family of Knocktopher, Co Kilkenny have bred Irish Draughts for over a century. Tom Hodgins, who more recently had the well known sire Roll On, bred Laughton (446). He was regarded as an influential jumping stallion. His sire Laughton's Last was bred by Tom Hodgins father and his sire, the first Laughton was bred by his uncle. Laughton himself sired three stallions, Bell Laughton from an Innishowen mare, Bally Laughton, out of a Glengariff mare and Lahinch, out of a Mount Leinster mare. The name Laughton comes from the place where Castlereagh actually stood.

Laughton's Last was Ikey Bell's hunter in England. He was also successful in point to points. He was returned to the Laughton yard in 1937 replacing the family's well known stallion Sentry. A Sentry mare was the great grandam of Boomerang, Eddie Macken's world famous showjumper. Royal Gem the thoroughbred maternal grandsire of Milestone also stood with Tom Hodgins.

Lahinch

Lahinch (558) foaled in 1963 a chesnut son of Laughton stood with Vincent Faughnan in Co Leitrim. His dam was Illane Imp (5365) by Mount Leinster (375). The best known of his ten stallion sons were **Merrygold** (644) bred from a Chilon (TB) mare, who produced Kildalton Gold (774); and **Dangan King** (613) who had two stallion sons Silver Laughton (662) and Dangan Boy (730). Another son is the 1985 Naldo (773) who is still on the stallion register.

Ginger Dick

Bell Laughton (578) was another of Laughton's three stallion sons. He bred Ginger Dick (643) a bay foaled in 1969 who produced Ballinrobe Boy (703) and Supreme Ginger (863) Ginger Dick was out of a Battleburn mare, Laughton Lass. He stood with Owen Hallinan, near Westport, Co Mayo. He had 442 registered foals.

Ballinrobe Boy

Ballinrobe Boy (703) is a 1977 chesnut son of Ginger Dick (643). His dam was Rose of Brackloon (8653) a daughter of Dickie a son of Barna (442) out of a mare with no recorded pedigree, Kilboyne Baroness (7035) He was bred by William O'Connell and is owned by Clara View Stud, the Curragh, Co Kildare. Ballinrobe Boy has bred successful showjumpers including Red Fire Thorn, Ebstree's Rose of Ireland, Ballyclare 2, Perfect Day, Radiush Again, Sunleyhill Biscuit,. Sir Richard, Whiteface and Hawkshead Epona. Amongst his eventers are Gatcombe Intermediate winner, Grace and Favour, advanced eventer, Briarlands Firewood who won the Wilton Horse Trials in 1999 and the intermediate eventer Ballinrobe Babe, His show progeny include the stallion Oranmore Boy, Snowford All Sun shine, Snowford Rupert and the part bred Marlay, a Windsor winner. Ballinrobe Boy is the sire of the stallion Attwood Black Laughton, who stands in England. Ballinrobe Boy has 94 registered foals.

Blue Rajah

Blue Rajah (759) a 1983 grey carries Laughton on his dam side. His dam Trinity (10341) was a daughter of Merrygold (644) and grand daughter of Lahinch son of Laughton. He is by Blue Peter (536) by Kylemore (459) by Irish Pearl (193). He was bred by Suma Stud and is owned by John and Sharon Alexander, Ballymena, Co Antrim who bought him as a foal and had him inspected as a three year old. He bred the championship mare The Blue Lady and her full brother, Touch of the Blues who bred six stallions in England before being exported to the USA.

Corrundulla Star

Corrundulla Star (740) is a 1980 chesnut who carries Laughton on his dam side. His dam Annaghdown (10147) is a grand daughter of Lahinch by The Galway Boy (659) Annaghdown's dam was Coolaghy Peggy an ISH mare by Erne's Pride (641). He was bred by Andrew Hennelly and stands with Colm Redmond, Avoca, Co Wicklow. He has 116 registered foals.

Castana

Castana (837) is a 1991 chesnut son of Naldo by Lahinch and a great grandson of Laughton. He is discussed in the section on King of Diamonds.

Celtic Gold

Celtic Gold (838) is a 1992 chesnut grandson of Lahinch. By Kildalton Gold by Merrygold his dam was Carnalway Lady (10758) by Clover Hill. Her dam was Branlugga Lady an AID mare by the thoroughbred Matchlike He was bred by John

Sandall and stands with Celtic Winners Ltd, Victoria, Australia. He has 55 registered foals in Ireland.

Classic Vision

Classic Vision (827) is a 1990 bay son of Ginger Dick by Bell Laughton out of Laughton Lass by Battleburn. His dam was Lady Glen (10384) by Flagmount Diamond a son of King of Diamonds. Her dam was Silver Rock (9115) by Drinagh Chieftain (606). He was bred by McLoughlin Brothers, Dundonald, Co Down, and stands with Trevor Badger in Co Westmeath. He jumped to Grade A. He has 29 registered foals. See section on King of Diamonds. .

Corran Ginger

Corran Ginger (812) is a 1989 chesnut son of Ginger Dick who was a son of Bell Laughton and grandson of Laughton. His dam was Diamonds Colleen (10679), a daughter of Kingsway Diamond and grand daughter of King of Diamonds. Her dam was Carrow Coleen by St Isodore (559). He was bred by Jack Perry and stands with Robert Davis, Ballybofey, Co Donegal. He has 123 registered foals.

Donovan

Donovan (859) is a 1991 grey son of Parnell who carries Laughton as the sire of his dam Kilshanny (6360). On his sire side Parnell goes back to Gortlee (426). Donovan's dam was Night Nurse 2 (10054) by Ben Purple. Her dam was Young Sweetheart an ISH mare by the thoroughbred Awkward Brief. Donovan was approved in the UK in 1994. He stands with Lawrence Flood, Rathangan, Co Kildare. He was bred by D. E Walton.

Ginger Holly

Ginger Holly (82) is a 1989 chesnut son of Ginger Dick, the

grandson of Laughton. His dam was Westfield Lass, a daughter of Flagmount Boy (663) and grand daughter of King of Diamonds. Her dam was Westfield Rose (9025) a daughter of Galtylara (548) He was bred by Peter McHugh and stands with Owen Hallinan, Westport, Co Mayo. He has 120 foals.

Gold Link

Gold Link (805) is a 1988 grey son of Merrygold by Lahinch and great grandson of Laughton. Merrygold's dam was Sheer Dynamite by the thoroughbred Chilon. Gold Link's dam was Cranny Starlight (7469) by Gleaming Light (575) by Cushnahouna (471). He was bred by Cecilia Delaney and stands with Keith Hatton, Kilkenny. He has 57 registered foals.

Herrero

Herrero (843) is a 1993 grey son of Kildalton Gold and great Grandson of Laughton. His dam was Brehans Pride (10979) by Pride of Toames (686) Her dam was Brehan Lass (10374) by Legaun Prince (660) by Pride of Shaunlara. He was bred by Chantal Deon and stands in the USA with Ann Dann, Florida. See section Irish Draughts in America.

Kildalton Gold

Kildalton Gold (774) was a 1985 chesnut son of Merrygold By Lahinch and great grandson of Laughton. His dam was Kildalton Countess (10180) a daughter of Ben Purple, out of Enniskeane Countess by Glen Lad (458) He was bred by Kildalton Agricultural College and stood with Thomas Kearns, Mooncoin, Co Kilkenny. He has 553 registered foals. See section on Ben Purple.

Merrymate

Merrymate (815) is a grey 1988 son of Merrygold (644) By Lahinch and great grandson of Laughton. His dam was Silver

Queen (8279) a daughter of Poulgorm (546) by Abbeylara (476) Her dam was Glanmire Light, no pedigree has been recorded. He was bred by Timothy Sullivan and stands with John Geoghegan, Ardrahan, Co Galway He has 235 registered foals.

Naldo

Naldo (773) a 1985 chesnut son Lahinch by Laughton is owned by Brendan Merrigan, Tipperary. His dam was the Mountain View mare Cora Belle who bred twelve foals up to 1995. Naldo was bred by Michael Duignan He has 48 registered foals.

Supreme Ginger

Supreme Ginger (863) by Ginger Dick (643) a 1995 bay son of Bell Laughton (578) is owned and was bred by Edwin McLoughlin, Newbliss, Co Monaghan. His dam was Anne Diamond (1074) by Flagmount Diamond (702) out of Fantane Anne (8269) He was Approved in 2000

Westmeath lad

Westmeath Lad (834) is a son of Kildalton Gold and is the fourth generation from Laughton in the sire line. His dam was Ireland's Diamond (10008) a daughter of King of Diamonds. Her dam was Tullagh's Ireland's Glory by Merrion (447) He was bred and is owned by Timothy Carey, Castletowngeoghegan, Co Westmeath. He has 71 registered foals

Sport Horse Stallions

Errigal Flight is a 1984 chesnut son of King of Diamonds out of the Highland Flight mare Highlight 2, an AID mare. She was a daughter of Laughton's Belle (8558) by Bell Laughton (578) one of the three stallion sons of Laughton (446).

Errigal Flight was bred by Eric Atkinson and stands with Wilfred Atkinson, Durrow, Co Laois. A popular stallion he has 367 registered foals.

Laughton's Flight is a full brother of Errigal Flight and stands with Tommy Brennan, Coolgrange House Stud, Co Kilkenny. Bred by Eric Atkinson, Leighlinbridge, Co Carlow he was foaled in 1983 and has been popular. He has 470 registered foals.

Millstreet Gold is another sport horse stallion with Laughton on the dam side. A 1986 bay son of the thoroughbred Sky Boy his dam was Parkmore Bella (8290) by Bell Laughton (578) by Laughton (446). He was bred by Patrick Wafer, Carnew, Co Wicklow. and stands with Tom Meagher, Kedrah House Stud, Cahir, Co Tipperary. He is owned by Hanna Nyholm, Harcourt, France

Slievenamon

Slievenamon (682) was a son of Ballinoe Boy (596) who was by an unknown thoroughbred sire out of a Clareman (429) mare. Ballinoe Boy stood only 15.3hh but was a quality horse. He was owned by the Ryan Lukes of Cappaghmore on the Limerick Tipperary border. Slievenamon's dam was George's Girl (5639) by Rusheen Hero (445). Clareman traces back to Comet, number one in the Irish Draught Horse Book. Rusheen Hero traces back to Young Arthur, number nine in the Irish Draught Horse Book on his sire side and to Young JP (12) in his dam pedigree.

Slievenamon was bought as a foal by Bobby Barton, Co Tipperary, and later stood with Gaynor Stapleton in Aughrim, Co Wicklow and with James McMahon, Ennis, Co Clare. He was an influential stallion and produced a number of stallion sons as well as the two special mares Fast Woman and Seafin Lady. Fast Woman was the dam of Fast Silver (829). He had 195 registered foals.

Elm Hill

Elm Hill (786) by Sillot Hill (735) is a grandson of Slievenamon out of the Clonmore Boy (576) mare Liscannor Grey (8599). Clonmore Boy was a son of the important stallion Tara (369) Elm Hill a grey foaled in 1986 was bred by John McMahon and stands with Bernard Kennelly, Cahermoyle, Ardagh, Co Limerick. He has 115 registered foals.

Red Hackle

Red Hackle (792), a chesnut son of Slievenamon out of the Sir Henry 11 mare Touree Girl (9058) was foaled in 1987. He was bred by John Godkin, Co Wicklow and stands with John Meehan, Riversdale, Gurteen, Ballymote, Co Sligo. He has 191 registered foals. His progeny includes the succcesful show hunter Enniskean foaled 1991 bred by David O'Brien.

Rockrimmon Silver Diamond

Rockrimmon Silver Diamond (846) is a 1994 grey son of SillotHill and grandson of Slievenamon. His dam was Saggart's Millie (11152) by Diamond Prince (726) a son of King of Diamonds. He was bred by Patrick Gleeson. He was exported to the United States and is owned by Allen Stout, North Carolina. See section Irish Draughts in America.

Sammy's Pride

Sammy's Pride (808) is a full brother to Red Hackle. A chesnut he was foaled in 1988. He was bred by John Godkin and stands with Samuel Codd, Tinahely, Co Wicklow. He has 36 registered foals.

Sillot Hill

Sillot Hill (735) is a chesnut son of Slievenamon and probably the most successful of his descendant stallions. He was bred from the Brandon Hill (517) mare Warren Lass (8719) and foaled in 1980. He was bred by Andy Fitzpatrick and stands with James McMahon, Ennis, Co Clare. He has 206 registered foals including Rockrimmon Silver Diamond.

Woodland Boy

Woodland Boy (826) by Oakley Dawn (715) is a chesnut grandson of Slievenamon out of the Silver Skip (729) mare

Woodhill Lass (10801). Foaled in 1990 he was bred by Frances Browne and is owned by Nora Niland, Balla, Co Mayo. He has 40 registered foals.

Slievenamon had two other stallion sons, O'Malley and Oakley Dawn both foaled in 1978. Oakley Dawn was a successful stallion and had 188 registered foals. Slievenamon has a current Sport Horse stallion, Kiltealy Boy, a black foaled 1980 who stands with Jay Bowe at Enniscorthy, Co Wexford.

Outcrosses

There are only a handful of outcross stallions in Ireland. The most important is undoubedly the Grade A showjumper and sire of Cruising, Seacrest, but his reputation is based more on his individual performance than the fact that he is an alternative bloodline. The Irish Draught world is concerned at the loss of old bloodlines, but the reality is that these bloodlines must have a strong performance bias if they are to attract the support of breeders. Seacrest now has two Approved stallion sons. Blue Rajah is an important outcross option and Huntingfield Rebel is performance bred. Donovan, the son of Parnell has been brought from England to stand in Kildare. Coolehane Flight, Golden Warrior, and Grange View all carry recent thoroughbred blood and clearly have only limited qualifications to represent old Irish Draught pedigrees.

Blue Rajah

Blue Rajah (759), a 1983 grey is by Blue Peter (536) by Kylemore (459) by Irish Pearl (193). He carries Laughton on his dam side (see chapter on Laughton). He was bred by Suma Stud and is owned by John and Sharyn Alexander, Ballymena, Co Antrim who bought him as a foal and had him inspected as a three year old. He bred the championship mare The Blue Lady and her full brother, Touch of the Blues who bred six stallions in England before being exported to the USA. The Alexanders also produced the important mare Seafin Lady which they bought as a four year old in Co Down. (See chapter The Showring).

In an article in the *Irish Draught Horse Yearbook 1997*

Sharyn Alexander describes how they decided to look at colts for use as stallions and short listed two. One was the eventual Blue Rajah which they saw in Carrickmacross where he was on grass. The other by Ben Purple was in Co Tipperary with Willie Burke who bred Seafin Lady. He was later the stallion Holycross. Blue Rajah was shown as a two year old at the National Show and won his class and went on to take the Young Horse championship. He has 119 foals.

Brown Lad Lara

Brown Lad Lara (758) is a 1979 son of Galtylara (548) by the controversial stallion Abbeylara out of a Glen Lad (458) mare Lomanaugh Peg (8036). Abbeylara was controversial because it was claimed there were two Abbeylaras, one of which was a substitute when the original died. There were allegations of Clydesdale breeding. It seems, however, that Clydesdale or not, the Abbeylara in the record books was fairly well regarded. Glen Lad was an important sire and produced the dams of a number of stallions, including Pride of Toames, Enniskeane Pride and Enniskeane Prince (dam Enniskeane Countess). Brown Lad Lara stands in Co Cork with Michael O'Regan of Rosscarbery. He was bred by Daniel Creedon. He has 60 foals.

Clonakilty Hero

Clonakilty Hero is a 1996 son of Brown Lad Lara who was performance tested and Approved in 2001. His dam was Cappanahola Ruby Anne by Grove Hero, a son of Rusheen Hero who, bred George's Girl, dam of Slievenamon and also the dam of Paul Darragh's international showjumper Heather Honey. Clonakilty Hero was champion foal at Clonakilty Show. He is owned by Eric Atkinson, Carlow. He was put up for sale at the Irish Draught National Show 2001 but was led out unsold at £12,000. He was bred in Cork by Humphrey Lynch.

Clonakilty Hero covered in the 2001 season.

Coolehane Flight

Coolehane Flight (782) is a 1985 bay son of Gold Coin (628) by Autumn Gold (TB) a son of Nearco. His dam is Slone (10333) by Wild Wave (560) a son of Gortlee (426) He was bred in Co Cork by David Purcell of Coolehane,Macroom and stands with John Shorten, Co Limerick. Gladys Nesbitt stood him for the 2000 season at Kilnacloy Stables, Co Monaghan. Coolehane Flight was presented for Approval as a three year old. He is a big bay horse 172 cms with 23 cms of bone. He was regularly hunted by his owner who describes him as an armchair ride. He breeds big quiet horses with brilliant temperament, easy to break and comfortable to ride. Gladys Nesbitt saw him in 1999 at a stallion parade at Mallow racecourse but David Purcell declined to sell him on this occasion. He subsequently changed his mind and Coolehane Flight moved to Co Monaghan in April 2000. He was sold on to John Shorten following the purchase of Agherlow by Gladys Nesbitt. Coolehane Flight produced The Corker, the Lightweight Hunter champion at Hickstead 2001. 80 foals.

Donovan

Donovan (859) is a 1991 grey son of Parnell (642) who stood with Bernard Stanford, Gort, Co Galway and subsequently went to England. Parnell is a son of Aughadown (565) by Gortlee (426) Parnell's dam was Kilshanny (6360) by Laughton (446). Donovan carries Ben Purple as the sire of his dam Night Nurse 2 (10054). (See chapter on Ben Purple . Donovan was approved in Britain in 1994. He was bred by De Walton and is owned by Lawrence Flood, Rathangan, Co Kildare.

Golden Warrior

Golden Warrior (752) is a 1981 chesnut son of Rathlin Star

(707) by Armada Star (566). His dam was Kylebeg Lass (10236) by Bawnlahan (585) out of the Blarney Castle mare Cousin Rachel (6053). Cousin Rachel bred in Galway by James Kennedy produced the stallion Clonfert. Golden Warrior stands with John Fahey in Claregalway. He has 306 foals.

Grange View

Grange View (750) is a 1981 chesnut son of Mountain View (638), the sire of Carrabawn View by Glen Star (478) His dam is Old Grange Lady (8839) by the thoroughbred Rex Gets Busy. He was bred by Gregory Feeney and stands with Ivan Kee in Co Donegal. He has produced jumpers. He has 78 foals.

Huntingfield Rebel

Huntingfield Rebel is the produce of two outcross lines. His sire was the Grade A Glenagyle Rebel (788) by Glenside (563) exported to Zimbabwe and his dam Whippy by Blue Peter was 1996 Supreme champion at the National Irish Draught show. He was brought back from England to stand at Suma Stud in Co Meath. He showjumped to Grade C and competed in dressage and cross country and was Reserve champion at the Irish Draught performance show at Greenhills in 1999. He won the Irish Draught stallion class at Dublin the same year. Foaled in 1990 he stands 16.3 hh. He was bred by Susan Lanigan O'Keeffe

Seacrest

Seacrest (728) is a 1979 grey son of Knockboy (700) by the Kerryman (492) Knockboy's dam was Arctic Lass ISH by Arctic Que, a thoroughbred sire who had an established reputation as a producer of jumpers. Seacrest's dam was Seaspray (655) by the important sire Tara (369). Seacrest, a Grade A showjumper, is the sire of the international jumping stallion

Cruising. He is discussed for convenience with Tara in the chapter on Clover Hill. Seacrest stands with Mary McCann in Co Kildare. He has 326 foals.

Seacrest's first stallion son to be registered was **Coolcronan Wood** (865) a 1996 grey who was Approved in 2000. His dam was Augusta's Vintage (11561) by Glenagyle Rebel out of an AID mare Ballyderney Rose. He was bred by Mrs Deborah McGuinness and produced by David Dodd, Coolcronan House, Foxford, Co Mayo. He stands with Timothy O'Regan, Mallow, Co Cork.

Sir Rivie a 1993 grey was Approved after performance testing in 2001. His dam is Ginger Anne (11210) by Ginger Dick (643) which brings in the Laughton line. Ginger Dick foaled in 1969 was a son of Bell Laughton, one of Laughton's three stallion sons. Ginger Dick himself was out of a Battleburn mare, Laughton Lass. He stood with Owen Hallinan near Westport, Co Mayo. Sir Rivie is owned by Sean Foley, Cloverhill, Co Sligo. He had 312 SJAI points at the time of inspection.

Sean Foley, a Sligo publican bought Sir Rivie as a foal from his breeder George Draper, a local auctioneer. He showed him successfully as a yearling and sent him jumping with John McGuinness as a four year old. McGuinness has been his pilot ever since. His showjumping career has been consistently successful and he went to Lanaken in 1999.

One of Sir Rivie's most striking characteristics is his ability in speed classes He won six in 2001 He will stay jumping and will cover mares by AI. Sean Foley already has a promising three year old by him. His first foal was sold at Cavan as a yearling for £3000.

Sport Horses

Consideration must be given to the role which the Irish Draught plays in the production of the Irish Sport Horse. The Irish Sport Horse Studbook has a separate classification for sport horses, the majority of which are a cross of thoroughbred and Irish Draught in either direction. There are very few competing Irish horses in any discipline which do not have some Irish Draught background in their make-up. Irish sport horse stallions (ISH) contribute some 27% of the annual Irish foal crop. The 2000 registered foal figure for ISH sires was 1200. Irish Draught sires contributed 825 foals of which 254 were purebred.

The arrival of the Continental stallions is putting pressure on both the thoroughbred and sport horse sires and like it or not, the Irish Draught as a breed has got to face the fact that performance is the key to modern horsebreeding. The registration of Irish Draught fillies is running at around 160 a year now, a relatively good total given that the number of purebred foals is so small. There are 992 Irish Draught active breeding mares.

Ireland has traditionally cross bred its performance horses. The thoroughbred horse on the mares of the countryside was the way to go for centuries. It was a successful recipe and under its aegis, the Irish horse achieved international renown in all spheres of equestrian sport. The sport horse stallions that stand today - there are about 70 on the Approved list - have produced sporting progeny whose performance is rarely equalled by pure bred Irish Draught stock.

The Irish Draught, although vastly different from the general run of horses with a strictly agricultural background is of its nature heavier and more a strongly boned than the competition horse. But it must not be forgotten that the Irish Draught has its own special inbuilt agility which contributes to the prowess of the part bred horse.

It has to be said, however, that the Irish Draught in its pure form is not a match for the tracks and standards of today's international competitions. Indeed the Irish horse in its entirety is having difficulty in competing with the Continental horses which is why so many showjumping people in particular are turning to imported sires to meet their needs for better jumpers. The future role of the ISH stallions with Irish pedigrees (the sons of foreign breds foaled in Ireland can also be admitted to the ISH stallion section) will be determined by their ability to persuade mare owners that the way forward lies with athletic Irish/thoroughbred bloodlines and not with the increasingly challenging continentals. The Irish Draught as a breed must ensure that it supplies as much of the 'Irish' ingredient as possible.

Standard Set by Coille Mor Hill

The question, of course, is whether the breed in general can reach the national standard established for instance by Coille Mor Hill, or indeed whether it really wants to go down this road. There are many breeders who do not see the Irish Draught as a performance breed in the showjumping sense and do not want to get involved in the more immediate thoroughbred crosses which this standard of athleticism entails.

The real question for the future, however, is whether the Irish Draught can survive as some kind of showring anachronism. Numbers have been steadily falling although it is maintained that there are mares out there which are entitled to registration but which have been precluded from so doing because their dams have not been inspected. The re-opening of the AID register in a limited way announced in early 2002 might improve the figures. An approach limited to securing numbers is clutching at straws. The real future for the Irish Draught lies in its ability to keep up with equestrian sport. Horsebreeding is an evolving business. One must ask if the Irish Draught is really keeping up with the game.

An aspect of the thinking behind the creation of the ISH classification in the stallion Approval process was that showjumping would eventually establish its own performance sire lines from the ranks of is competing horse. This, of course, would depend on a substantial number of entires actually competing at top levels in showjumping, or at least demonstrating in performance testing their own individual ability to jump. There are many in the Irish Draught world who are opposed to the principle of performance testing Irish Draughts, although the standard set is pretty trivial. A mere ten showjumping points allows an Irish Draught to be considered. The day will come when mares will have to be performance tested in this country as well. This is the route which all European horse breeding nations have gone down.

Will the Irish Draught mare be able to stand up to this scrutiny. There is no reason to believe that the majority of useful three year old Irish Draught mares would not come through such a process. Realistically the mare that cannot jump a novice track is not worth breeding from in this day and age. Such mares should be excluded. The Irish Draught may present a splendid picture at its annual breed show with the mares and youngstock glistening in the summer sunlight but a more concise picture will have to be painted. To survive the Irish Draught must renew its role in Irish horsebreeding. To do so entails taking a real grip on the performance nettle.

Performance and conformation should go hand in hand in assessing horses, stallions or mares, for registration. This may mean coming to terms with a lighter type of horse, but these have already arrived. Coille Mor Hill, Classic Vision and Crosstown Dancer are cases in point. There is, of course a need to preserve standards of bone and substance for future outcrossing. The IDHS has a particular role to play in this regard. Too much emphasis on tradition, however, will be self defeating. The Irish Draught is no longer an agricultural horse. It is set up as a foundation for the Irish horse industry. It must adjust to meet the needs of that industry.

King of Diamonds has twenty descendant sport horse stallions and Clover Hill has twelve. Between them these two giants of the Irish Draught performance world account for half of the Approved Sport Horse sires. These figures clearly illustrate the dependence of the Irish horse industry on the Irish Draught. But it must be remembered that the people who count at the end of the day, the sport horse breeders, the buyers and above all the showjumping owners no longer have the faith in the breed as a fountain of performance. The Irish Draught has taken a hammering. The way forward has to be a realistic assessment of where supporters want to see it positioned in the years ahead.

Descendant Sires by King of Diamonds

The most popular of King of Diamonds descended sport horse sires are Laughton's Flight with 470 registered foals, Coevers Diamond Boy 417 foals, Highland King 394 foals, Kings Servant 389 foals, Errigal Flight 386 foals and the showjumping horse Puissance 284 foals.

Laughtons Flight

Laughton's Flight is a 1983 chesnut son of King of Diamonds out of the Highland Flight mare Highlight 2 (AID). He is discussed in the section on Laughton.

Errigal Flight

Errigal Flight is a 1984 full brother to Laughton's Flight. See Laughton section also.

Coevers Diamond Boy

Coevers Diamond Boy is a 1989 grey son of Diamond Lad by King of Diamonds out of the American bred Coevers (TB) mare Lochnavar Lady. There is no further dam pedigree. Coevers was a son of Nantullah by Nasrullah He was bred by Christopher Callinan and is owned by Thomas Brennan, Scarriff, Co Clare.

Highland King

Highland King is a 1975 chesnut son of Highland Flight (TB) and carries King of Diamonds on his dam side. His dam was Aishling out of a mare called Miss Wilson with no further recorded pedigree. He stands at Slyguff Stud. He was bred by Tom O'Neill. He was the first of the halfbred sons of King of Diamonds to go on the stallion register.

Kings Servant

Kings Servant is a 1981 chesnut son of King of Diamonds out of the Highland Flight mare Julie Anne 2. Her dam was Miss Wilson. He is owned by Slyguff Stud and was bred by Tom O'Neill.

Puissance

Puissance is a 1988 bay son of Slyguff Stud's important thoroughbred jumping stallion Imperius. His dam was Lady Marlane a daughter of Diamonds are Trumps by King of Diamonds. His grand dam was Mythical Times by the thoroughbred Mythical Sprite. Puissance was a competitive showjumper and has produced jumping progeny. He is owned by Stephen Lanigan O'Keeffe and stands with Michael Hutchinson, Gowran, Co Kilkenny. He was bred by James Whitty who sold him to Stephen Lanigan O'Keeffe as a foal.

Descendant Sires by Clover Hill

Most of Clover Hill's descendant sire progeny are much younger than their King of Diamonds counterparts. The majority of them are competing showjumpers and those which are eventually the most successful must surely have something to offer to Irish Draught performance breeding by a return to the studbook, although this suggestion does not find any favour with the Irish Draught authorities.

Boherdeal Clover

Boherdeal Clover brown 1992 ex Virginia Wolfa (ISH) by Regular Guy (TB) is owned by Pauric Goonan, Boherdeal House Stud, Crinkle, Birr, Co Offaly. He was Approved after performance testing in 1996 with 61 SJAI points. This horse made two appearancess in Lanaken and won the Harp Classic competition at Cavan in 1997 adding to the National Discovery title he won as a four year old and the IHB championship won in 1996.

The stallion only competed at about a dozen shows in 1997 but he got to the jump off in most of the major championships ridden by Brendan Ryan. He was then campaigned by Billy Twomey in Britain and won international and national classes.

He was leased to the Irish Army in 2000 and is ridden by Captain Gerry Flynn. Boherdeal Clover was bred by Pamela Miller, Mount Cashel, County Roscommon.

His dam Virginia Wolfa had a successful showing career as a foal, wining at Rathdowney and Piltown. She was placed sixth out of fifty three contenders in the All Ireland Filly Foal championships at Ballinasloe. She won a number of championships as a yearling two year old and three year old. She won the Bank of Ireland Brood mare championship at Sligo as a three year old. She won the Equitec Breeders Championship in Dublin in 1998 with a Diamond Lad foal at foot. She has produced a number of showjumping progeny.

Her sire Regular Guy who stood with Alo Tynan at Pike of Rushall was a winner over one and a half miles in England and placed four times from six starts including the White Rose Stakes (Group 3) and Wooditton Stakes. He ran in the English Derby in 1974. Retired to stud in 1976 he produced point to point and National Hunt winners. He was the sire of the USA's 1992 Olympic individual bronze medalist at Barcelona.

His sire Right Royal V won the French Derby, King George VI and Queen Elizabeth Stakes. He appears in numerous classic pedigrees as maternal grandsire. He is the paternal grandsire of Party Politics, Grand National winner and also of Kambalda, a well known racehorse and sire of numerous National Hunt winners.

Virginia Wolfa's dam Golden Pheasant was a liver chesnut standing 16.3hh. She won numerous prizes for her owner Patrick Jordan of Mountmellick. Golden Pheasant's sire Zolferine produced Paul Darragh's Grade A showjumper For Sure and other showjumpers. He traces in his sire line to

Tourbillon, an important influence on many international jumping lines.

Captain Clover

Captain Clover, brown, 1991, out of the thoroughbred mare Merlina by Falcon, a son of Milesian, owned by Gabriel Slattery Irishtown, Claremorris, Co Mayo, was Approved following performance testing in October 1997. His dam Merlina was retired from racing due to injury and retained for breeding due to her jumping technique and pedigree. He had 81 foals registered after the 2000 registration. He was Grade B in 2000, and represented the ISH Studbook at the World Breeding Federation championships at Lanaken where he was eighth from 106 starters. He is a winner of the All Ireland Showjumping Championship

Clover Brigade

Clover Brigade 1990 bay ex Brigade Princess by Light Brigade (TB) is owned by William Walsh, The Galross Stud, Borrisokane, Co Tipperary and is home bred. He was Approved in 1996 with 78 SJAI points. At the 2000 registration he had 286 foals registered. He is a full brother to the older Clover Valley.

Clover Echo

Clover Echo bay 1989 ex Moycullen by Blue Cliff (TB) out of anISH mare Autumn Bloom (1105442) is owned by Max Hauri This horse has 23 points in Ireland and has been placed and was a winner in national competitions in Switzerland in 1996. He was Approved in 1996 He was bred by Martin Murphy.

Clover Flush

Clover Flush, ch, 1991, ex The Queen of Trumps by King of

Diamonds out of ISH mare Carrigbrahan Peggy was owned and bred by Carmel Ryan, Waterford. He was Approved after performance testing in 1996 with 64 SJAI points. Clover Flush was sold in October 1997 for a substantial sum to Ian Mouser of Melbourne.

The grandam Carrigbrahan Peggy has produced five Grade A showjumpers and a current international. Carmel Ryan has spent thirty years developing a performance breeding enterprise based on a dam line going back to an unregistered Irish Draught called Bright Paddy. Carrigbrahan Peggy herself was a daughter of Carrigbrahan Lady by Seven Bells (TB) out of an unnamed Irish Draught mare by Bright Paddy.

Farney Clover

Farney Clover ex thoroughbred Farney Princess by Pitman is owned by William Walsh, The Galross Stud, Borrisokane, Co Tipperary. This 1990 chesnut is a son of Farney Princess a thoroughbred registered in the IHR by Pitman out of Brave Reward He was bred by Patrick Walsh. After the 2000 registration he had 303 foals recorded.

Le One

Le One ex Culbeg by Leabeg is a 1995 bay owned by Patricia Rowley, Culmore, Swinford, Co Mayo. He was reserve champion three year old at Goresbridge 1998. He was Approved in 1999. At the foal registration in 2000 he had 18 foals recorded.

Moore's Clover

Moore's Clover bay 1993 ex Beautiful Lily by Golden Cliff is owned by George Moore, Dysart, Ballinasloe, Co Galway. Moore's Clover is a Grade A showjumper. His dam Beautiful Lily was bred from a Frenchwood mare. She bred two other showjumpers, one of which is Wild Clover. Moore's Clover is classified as a small horse stallion. He qualified for loose jumping at Millstreet as a four year old and Dublin as a five year old. He won at Galway show in 1994. and won the McDonalds 153 cms class at Dublin in 1997. He has produced showring prizewinners. He has 33 foals recorded.

White Clover

White Clover ex Vanessa is owned by Gabriel Slattery Castlelawn, Stud, Dunmacreena, Irish Town, Claremorris, Co Mayo. This 1990 chesnut was Approved in 1993. He is out of a Kaiser (TB) mare Vanessa who goes back to Wily Trout (TB) a and a five year old recognised all round performer. White Clover had 470 foals recorded after the 2000 registrations. He reached Grade A after a small number of shows. He was a finalist in the Young Irelander as a four year old and qualified for the Goresbridge Young Horse championship as a three year old. He has had a good record jumping to date and qualified for the RDS both as a four year old

White Clover is the sire of showing winners, including supreme champions. He has produced finalists at the All Ireland Foal championships from 1997 to 2000 and he has been well represented at the three year old loose jumping performance class at the RDS and the Young Irelander at Millstreet. His progeny were were placed at both the RDS and Millstreet in 1998, 1999 and in 2000. In 1999 a White Clover gelding was Reserve Champion at the RDS. The fifth place also went to a White Clover. Another took fifth place at the Young Irelander finals at Millstreet. A four year old finished fifth in the National Discovery at Millstreet and was winner of the four year old division of the American Hunter at the RDS and also took the overall championship.

Special Mares

While the focus of attention is inevitably directed towards the stallions, there are many special mares which have played an equally important part in the development of the Irish Draught. The ordinary broood mare carries the future of the breed on her back and the majority of these attract little attention. They do their job, hopefully produce an economic foal and look forward to the next. Their owners probably keep them more from sentiment than from any real hope of making their breeding enterprise a honeypot. Occasionally, of course, a youngster comes forward that attracts attention, brings some acclaim to its breeder and makes the effort worth while. The show mares inevitably attract the limelight but there have been very special mares indeed which have never been groomed to come under the judge's scrutiny, but have made very important contributions to the development of the breed.

The economics of horsebreeding dictate that many of these mares are put to thoroughbred stallions but their owners conscious of the need to produce Irish Draught progeny as well often vary their sires ensuring that their mares do their bit to ensure the continuance of the breed. Fertility is a byword in Irish Draught breeding, many mares produce a minimum of a dozen foals during their careers, some of them a great many more. However, there have been and are still many empty years pinpointing the fact perhaps that in the past many mare owners, and indeed stallion owners too, failed to practice elementary husbandry by ensuring that the mares were clean at the time of covering.

Enniskeane Countess

The most important mare of recent times was probably Kildalton Countess. She was Kildalton Agricultural College's lady bountiful and produced several stallion sons. She is discussed in the section devoted to Ben Purple. Her dam Enniskeane Countess by Glen Lad (458) was an important mare as well, not just for the production of her famous daughter but for her stallion sons. Enniskeane Countess was bred by Billy Cotter, destined to be one of the most dedicated and influential members of the Irish Draught Horse Society, in Co Cork. Enniskeane Countess won the revived Irish Draught mare class at Dublin Horse Show in 1967 and eventually went to Kildalton. She bred Enniskeane Prince by Pride of Shaunlara (636) who showjumped in Britain and became a successful stallion. His full brother Enniskeane Pride also stood in Britain. Glen Lad bred the dams of several stallions.

Writing in the 2001 edition of the Irish Draught Horse Yearbook Billy Cotter recounts how he came to own Enniskeane Countess as a foal. He had in fact bought her full sister in 1957. She was bred from a well, known mare Valley Moon by Galty Og out of a Lough Derg dam, owned by Denis Lucey The sire of both fillies was of course Glen Lad. It had been Billy Cotter's ambition to get a mare with Woodranger breeding and this was as close as he could get. However, he sold the filly four years later and went back to Denis Lucey to buy another foal from Valley Moon. As it happened the mare had died and the foal was orphaned. Billy struck a deal with denis Lucey for thirty three pounds ten shillings. He brought her to the Irish Draught inspections as a three year old and got his life certificate in the name of Enniskeane Countess.

She was not an easy breeder but Billy persevered with her. In 1967 the Royal Dublin Society invited him to bring a mare to the revived Irish Draught class which was being brought back aftert a lapse of forty two years. So Enniskeane Countess made the long journey from West Cork to Dublin and brought home the red rosette. He turned down an offer of £1200 from an American lady but eventually agreed to sell her to Kildalton Agricultural College for £1500. There was a proviso that he would have an option on the first filly. This was Kildalton Rose which gave Billy back the pedigree which led to the success of Enniskeane Flash at Dublin Horse Show in 2001.

Gowran Betty

Gowran Betty was owned by Martin Brophy, of Flagmount, Co Kilkenny. A grey daughter of New Chieftain she was bred in Co Cork in 1967 and stood 16 hands. New Chieftain (508) was a chesnut son of Errigal foaled in 1958. There is no recorded pedigree on the dam side. His dam was Elgin (4549) by Killaloe (347). Errigal is an important influence here. He was also the sire of King of Diamonds. Killaloe was by Bright Ray (144) by Sunbeam (55) Sunbeam was a son of Comet, number one in the Irish Draught Horse Book. The sire of Bright Ray's unnamed dam was Defender number two in the book. His dam was the Dublin Guard (86) mare Muinessa (2058). Killaloe was a grey foaled in 1941 who stood with John O'Toole, Carnew, Co Wicklow. Dublin Guard was a son of Irish Guard (13) of son of Prince Henry (5). His dam was Shannon Lass (486) by Green Drake by Wild Rover

Gowran Betty had very old Irish Draught pedigree stretching back beyond the first registrations in 1918. She also carried the performance of Galty Boy (94) through Errigal's sire Silvermines (348).

Gowran Betty produced three King of Diamonds stallion sons, Flagmount Boy (683) foaled in 1974, Flagmount Diamond

(702) 1976, and Flagmount King (747) 1976.

Annaghmore Lass 2

Annaghmore Lass 2 (9040) brown 1974 by Gratin (TB) out of Annaghmore Lass (ISH) by Grackle (494) Bred by Bartley Cosgrove, Co Galway. Owned by JJ Harte, Co Fermanagh. Annaghmore Lass 2 bred fourteen foals between 1978 and 1996.

April Lass

April Lass (10324) 1978 chesnut by Skippy (688) out of Carrowmore Daisy (6957) by Knockanagow (600) bred by Michael J McLean, Co Mayo. Owner PJ Fitzpatrick, Co Laois. April Lass bred twelve foals between 1982 and 2000 including the stallion Cream of Diamonds (780) by Kingsway Diamond (736) bred by Thomas Niland, Co Mayo.

Ashling 2

Ashling 2 (8537) 1971 chesnut by King of Diamonds (547) out of Miss Wilson. Bred by Tom O'Neill, Slyguff Stud. She bred fifteen foals including the stallions Highland King (ISH) 1975 by Highland Flight (TB) her first foal. In 1992 she bred Kings Master (ISH) by Master Imp TB.

Ballydaly Lady

Ballydaly Lady (9162) 1970 bay by Bright as Gold (TB) bred by Jerry Corkery, Cork Owner John O'Connor, Cork. Ballydaly Lady bred fourteen foals between 1974 and 1994.

Bawnlahan Beauty

Bawnlahan Beauty (7752) was a 1968 grey daughter of Gortlee (426) out of Sarue Beauty by Pride of Bantry. She was bred by Jeremiah Lawlor, Co Cork. Bawnlahan Beauty won the Greenvale Mare Championship at Millstreet in 1978. She bred seven foals of which two became Approved stallions, Kingsway Diamond (736) by King of Diamonds bred by Frances Hatton and foaled in 1980 and Jack of Diamonds (743) also by King of Diamonds. Kingsway Diamond was brought to New Zealand by Thady Ryan.

Boston Burglar

Boston Burglar (6440) 1964 grey by Thoroughbred Prefairy out of Outer Limits by Ballycotton (432) out of Sun Star mare bred by Patrick Hoolin, Co Tipperary. She bred twelve foals. Her first foal was the stallion Pride of Shaunlara (636) by Milestone (498). foaled in 1969. In 1989 she produced the stallion Dunkerrin Grey Mist (809) by Carrabawn View (751).

Cap Hinch

Cap Hinch (8776) 1970 chesnut by Lahinch (558) bred by Patrick McGirl, Co Leitrim. Bred seventeen foals from 1974 to 1994.

Carlisheen Molly

Carlisheen Molly (10213) grey 1975 by Solo Head (464) out of Miss Gethins (8786) by Bally Laughton (579) bred by John A Cogan, Co Sligo. Owned by Suma Stud, Co Meath. Carlisheen Molly bred fifteen foals between 1980 and 1995

Carrigbawn Colleen

Carrigbawn Colleen (9418) was a grey daughter of Ben Purple (580) out of Flirty Gertie (8028) by Gortlee out of Irish Sun set (5471) by Irish Pearl (183) out of Black Beauty. She was foaled in 1974 and bred by Samuel Kingston in Co Cork. She bred ten foals, three of which became Approved stallions. These were Riverbank (748) by Kintara (696), Diamond King (756) by The Conqueror (725) and

Silver Glider (770) also by The Conqueror. These three stallions were bred by Daniel J Crowley, Co Cork.

Celtic Banner

Celtic Banner (8234) 1970 grey by Young Ireland (526) out of Marita (6476) by Kylemore Lad. Owner Noel C Hamilton, Co Wicklow. Celtic Banner bred eleven foals between 1976 and 1990 including the stallion Silver Granite (762) by Glenvara (706) owned by Fintan Flannelly. Silver Granite won the Irish Draught class in Dublin, was exported to the United States and later returned to Ireland to stand again with Fintan Flannelly.

Churchfield Champion

Churchfield Champion (7720) 1968 chesnut by Sang Froid (TB) . Owner John O'Sullivan, Co Tipperary. Churchfield Champion bred fourteen foals between 1973 and 1992.

Cora Belle,

Cora Belle (9415) 1975 chesnut by Mountain View (638) out of Lercarrow Daisy (8459) by Boherbue (544) out of Magher Girl (7421) Owner Eugene Owens, Co Monaghan. Cora Belle bred twelve foals from 1978 to 1995 including the stallion Naldo (773) by Lahinch (558). Bred by Michael Duignan.

Coronea Kilkee

Coronea Kilkee (9167) 1972 chesnut by Atlantic Boy (527) out of Willow Maid bred by Christy Haugh, Co Clare. Coronea Kilkee bred fourteen foals between 1975 and 1992.

Corran Lass 2

Corran Lass 2 (10189) by Ben Purple (558) out of Corran

Lake (8687) by Shandrum Prince (534) Bred by Patrick McCarthy Co Cork. Owner Ted O'Driscoll, Co Cork. Corran Lass 2 bred fourteen foals between 1980 and 1992.

Fast Woman

Fast Woman (10289)1978 grey by Slievenamon (682) out of Hard and Fast (6254) by Kantogher Pride (455) bred by Charles Lawless, Co Tipperary. Fast Woman won the Greenvale Championship in 1983, 1984 and 1988. She was owned by Sean Walshe of Knockboy Stud, Thurles, Co Tipperary. She was a prolific breeder and produced thirteen foals including the stallion Fast Silver (829) 1991 grey by Silver Hunter (681).

Garrynagree Moll

Garrynagree Moll (9067) grey 1970 by Brandon Hill (517) out of Brown Beauty. Bred by James Mulhall, Co Tipperary. Owner Michael Monaghan, Co Galway. Garrynagree Moll bred seventeen foals between 1974 and 1991.

Grey Beauty

Grey Beauty (10258) grey 1973 by Sir Henry 2 (614) Owned by Mrs William Bradford, Co Down. Grey Beauty bred sixteen foals between 1977 and 1996.

Grey Curragong

Grey Curragong (10604) 1983 grey by The Conqueror (725) out of Rena Grand (7761) by Rathlin out of Black Beauty, Bred by Michael Mennis, Co Cork and owned by Anna Kennedy, Co Kerry. Bred nine foals from 1987 to 1998 including sport horse stallion Leeside Ranger 1989 ch by Silverstone and O'Leary's Irish Diamond 1994 grey by Glidawn Diamond (754) exported to the USA.

Ireland's Diamond

Ireland's Diamond (10008) 1976 grey by King of Diamonds out of Tullagh Ireland's Glory (6653) by Merrion (447) out of Gort Polly. Owned and bred by Timothy Carey, Castletowngeoghegan, Co Westmeath. Bred eleven foals including stallions Westmeath Lad (834) 1991 ch by Kildalton Gold (774) and Star Kingdom (856) 1994 by Annaghdown Star (791).

Moneen Lady

Moneen Lady (8908) 1972 chesnut by Young Ireland (526) out of Lisdeen Lady. Bred by Michael Blake, Co Clare. Owner Patrick Clohessy, Co Clare. Moneen Lady bred fifteen foals from 1975 to 1994.

Moyglass Lass 2

Moyglass Lass 2 (8383) by Goleen (584) Bred by James Gunning, Co Galway. Owned by Tina Bogenberger, Co Clare. Moyglass Lass 2 bred sixteen foals from 1974 to 1993.

Night Nurse 2

Night Nurse 2 (10054) 1976 grey by Ben Purple (580) out of Young Sweetheart (ISH) by Awkward Brief out of Old Sweetheart (7281) by Gortlee (426) bred by John Tobin, Co Cork. This mare was exported to England but is the dam of two stallions which were registered in the UK but have returned to stand in Ireland. These are Glenlara (847) by Enniskeane Pride (717) and Donovan (859) 1991 by Parnell (642).

Nora 2

Nora 2 (9103) 1971 brown by Dove 2 (591) by Milestone out of Ballyglass Bess, bred by Sean Jones, Co Clare and owned EJ McNamara, MRCVS, Co Down. This is one of the most prolific brood mares in the studbook producing eighteen foals with only one year since 1977 without a foal. She bred the stallion RNE Shore (767) 1983 by Ireland's Pride (705). Undoubtedly the professional expertise of her owner played a part in her long and successful career as a brood mare. In 1997 and 1998 she was owned by Edward Laverty, Co Down

Parkmore Jewel

Parkmore Jewel a grey 1981 by Atlantic Boy 527) out of Derryfrench Rose (7398) by Laughton (446) bred by Paul Geoghegan, Co Galway. This mare bred seven foals and was successfully shown by her owner Patrick Wafer, Carnew, Co Wicklow. She bred three stallions, Parkmore Night (ISH) 1987 by Carnival Night, Parkmore Pride (841)1991 by Pride of Shaunlara, and Carrick Gold (ID) 1992 by Kildalton Gold (774) showjumper.

Pluma

Pluma (8697) Bay 1971 by Ben Purple (580) out of Enniskean Winner. Bred by Dennis Driscoll, Co Cork Owner Robert McIlroy, Co Tyrone. Pluma bred fourteen foals between 1974 and 1994.

Seaview Lass

Seaview Lass (10110) 1974 chesnut by Colman (612) out of Sea View Grainne (7433) by Cheyne (TB). Bred by Sebastian King, Co Mayo. Sea View Lass bred eight foals from 1978 to 1994 including the stallions Sandyhill Boy (739) by Skippy (688) and Carrabawn View (751) by Mountain View (638) both bred by Sebastian King.

Shauna

Shauna (10240) 1977 roan by Pride of Shaunlara (636) out of Gloun Rose (8887) by Ben Purple (580). Bred by John

McCarthy, Co Cork. Shauna bred eight foals including three stallions, Shauna's Diamond (7869) ch 1984, by Diamonds are Trumps (711), Trumpet Major (794) ch 1987 and Shauna's Pride by Ireland's Pride (705), all bred by Michael Gavin, Co Westmeath. Shauna was a successful show mare.

Tara Sky

Tara Sky (10499) 1983 grey is a full sister to Whippy. She was bred by Susan Lanigan O'Keeffe and is owned by Fintan Branigan. She bred ten foals from 1987 to 1999. She is the dam of the Grade A stallion Crosstown Dancer (821) by Flagmount Diamond (702). He stands at Suma Stud.

Thunder Girl

Thunder Girl (11151) 1985 bay by Diamond Lad (695) out of Corlisheen Beauty (10375) by Mountain View (638) out of Corker Del (ISH) by Lahinch (558) out of Corker Grey (8502) by Milestone (498) Bred by John A Cogan, Co Sligo, owned by Padraig Clarke, Co Galway. Bred eight foals from 1990 to 2000 including stallion Finn's Clover Inn (850)1995 by Clover Hill (665). Mackney Clover by Clover Hill was approved as a stallion in 2001.

Townrath Rose

Townrath Rose (10182) 1975 chesnut by Skylark (627) out of Garrybawn Queen (8209) by Cascius (TB) out of Garrybawn Princess (6621) Bred By Aloysius Duffy, Co Monaghan. Owner Noel Norris, Co Louth. Townrath Rose bred fourteen foals between between 1978 and 1997.

Whippy

Whippy (10426) 1981 grey by by Blue Peter (536) out of Softee (10243) by Skylark (627) out of Goodness Gracious 2 (7933) by Cheyne (TB) out of Irish Molly (5789). Owned by

Susan Lanigan O'Keeffe, Co Meath. Bred nine foals from 1986 and produced jumpers. She bred a stallion son Huntingfield Rebel (836) 1990 grey by Glenagyle Rebel (788) who was exported to England and returned to stand at Suma Stud. Whippy was 1996 Supreme Champion at the national Irish Draught Show.

The Showring

The showring has been the public face of the Irish Draught since the revival drive began in 1976. In particular the Greenvale Championship staged at Millstreet Show each year from 1977 until late in the eighties was the focal point of publicity for the breed. Greenvale champions were hailed as the best of breed and for the first few years at least, the class set the Irish Draught world alight. There was a well endowed prize fund and up to thirty qualifiers were staged throughout Ireland and the mares and their owners made the long journey to Ireland's second most important horse show after Dublin without complaint.

The first winner was Patrick Duane's Pink Carnation, a daughter of Goleen out of the Merrion mare White Carnation. Bawnlahan Beauty by Gortlee out of a Pride of Bantry mare Sarue Beauty headed the lineup the following year and a procession of quality mares followed year after year. Some mares captured the title more than once. Fast Woman by Slievenamon out of the Kantogher Pride mare Hard and Fast won in 1983 and 1984. Bundrameen Lass, a daughter of Ben Purple out of the Glen of Aherlow mare Bundrameen Dolly won in 1985 and 1986. Slievenamon saw a second daughter Seafin Lady out of the Milestone mare Dan's Pride win in 1987. The Laughton bloodlines received the accolade on two successive occasions with Ballybane Grace by Aughadown out of the Laughton mare Golden Wedding winning in 1979 and Doonmore Damsel by Atlantic Boy out of the Laughton mare Willow Maid the victor in 1980.

There were other outlets. The annual national breed show became a major success moving to different venues around the country after its debut days at Suma Stud and the classes at Dublin Horse Show began to fill up. No one who saw the crush of entries at Dublin in 2001 could fail to be impressed by the dedication of breeders who the previous week had travelled to the wonderful venue of Necarne Castle in Co Fermanagh for the national show and turned out again for Dublin. There were all Ireland foal championships and special brood mare championships. Showing became a way of life for many breeders, although very often the really hard working brood mares which produced foals year after year were seldom seen outside their own farms.

Anna Liffey

Anna Liffey (10626) 1982 grey by Sir Henry 2 (614) out of Annabella (6539) by Clareman (429) bred and owned by Pat O'Neill, Celbridge was Supreme champion at the national show in 1989. Bred four foals up to 1999.

Alice 4

Alice 4 (9089) by Zolferine (TB) 1970 bay bred and owned by Fintan Flannelly, Kill, Co Kildare and also by Ronnie McCombe, Co Dublin. Bred ten foals from 1978 to 1996. Alice was a major winner of showing classes on the east coast. She was more halfbred in type than Irish Draught and generally went down in classes where true Irish Draughts were competing. Her foals were all good jumpers.

April Storm

April Storm (10419) by Blue Peter (5360) out of Silver Dawn 2 (10231) bred and owned by Charlotte and Nigel Moore, Co Antrim. April Storm bred eleven foals from 1984 to 1998. April Storm was an outstanding mare. Her dam

Silver Dawn demonstrated the traditional versatility of the real Irish Draught, being ridden, hunted and driven in shafts and chains She competed in the Utility Class at the Spring Show in Dublin and at Balmoral Show. She won the revived Irish Draught class at Balmoral in 1979 from 24 mares and was champion broodmare at the first Irish Draught National Show at Suma Stud in 1985.

April Storm was Silver Dawn's first purebred foal and was registered as an in foal mare at two years. She was shown under saddle and hunted and competed in dresage in any season when she was not in foal. She was National Broodmare Champion at the national breed show in 1990, twice RID champion broodmare at the RDS in 1986 and 1988, and twice champion at Balmoral. She also won the Leitrim Breeders Championship and the Best Young Mare at Milllstreet in 1984. She was a prizewinner at shows throughout Ireland. Her foals were all successful and included My Hilltop Lady 1992, winner of the Irish Draught Yearling filly championship and also as a two year old. She also won the Limerick Lady Championship and won at the RDS and RUAS in 1996. Her 1995 filly Tullys Mist won the All Ireland national championship as a yearling and two year old. She was also a winner at the RDS and the national show in 1999.

April Storm was a tall striking mare standing about 16.3 hh Charlotte Moore says she was a superb mare to ride across country and passed her ability on to her progeny. Her bloodline continues in her daughters through the female line. She did not produce any purebred colts.

Ballybane Grace

Ballybane Grace (7846) by Aughadown (565) out of Golden Wedding by Laughton grey 1968 owned by Bernard Stanford

Gort, Co Galway. Winner of Greenvale Championship. Bred eight foals from 1974 to 1986 including stallion Grey Macha (746) by Pride of Toames (686)

Ballycoolan Silver and Gold

Ballycoolan Silver and Gold (11495) 1992 grey by Kildalton Gold (774) out of Hard Silver (10706) by Silver Hunter (681) out of Hard and Fast (6254) by Kantogher Pride (455) Bred and owned by Vivienne Bradley, Co Laois.

Bawnlahan Beauty

Bawnlahan Beauty (7752) 1968 grey by Gortlee (426) out of Sarue Beauty. Bred by Jeremiah Lawlor, Cork. Owned by David Hatton, Carlow. See chapter Special Mares.

Brehan Lass

Brehan Lass (10374) 1979 grey by Legaun Prince (660 out of Brehan Lass 2 (9239) by Kilcolman (538) Bred by Sarah Campbell, Limerick and owned by Chantal Deon. Kerrygold championship winner. Brehan Lass is the dam of Brehan's Pride a successful mare in her own right. Chantal Deon bought Brehan Lass in 1981 after she had failed the RID mare inspection in Limerick, an extraordinary lapse for what was later to become an outstanding mare. She went hunting with the local hounds, Galway Blazers, North Galway and East Galway as a four year old. She carried on hunting and successfully showjumping until 1986. She competed as a Grade B at Dublin Horse Show before being sent to the stallion for the first time. Mrs Deon received an offer from Swiss buyers but decided to keep her for breeding.

Brehan Lass began a breeding and showing career in 1987 producing fourteen foals including Brehan's Pride. Other foals were Bran Flake, jumping and breeding in Portugal, Hermine jumping in the USA, Tynagh Gold, a Grade A showjumper and winner of the six year old championship at Dublin Horse Show in 1998. Cradilo by KIldalton Gold, an approved stallion was Irish Draught Performance Champion USA 1998 and Irish Draught A!l over North America Champion the same year. In her showing career from 1987 to 1993, Brehan Lass won sixty four first prizes, including the Millstreet championship, and seventeen second prizes

Brehan's Pride

Brehan's Pride (10979) 1988 grey by Pride of Toames (686) out of Brehan Lass (10374) by Legaun Prince (660) bred and owned by Chantal Deon, Tynagh, Loughrea, Co Galway. A daughter of Brehan Lass. Selected for Quality Brood mare status winner of 1996 Aer Rianta championship winner and All Ireland Mare Championship 1996. The following year she won seventeen first prizes including Balmoral. She won ninety nine first prizes, seventeen seconds and six thirds in her showing career. Brehan's Pride bred seven foals between 1992 and 2001 four of which were stallions. One of these Herrero stands in Florida. He won fifteen first prizes as a foal and with his dam captured the Breeders Reserve Championship at Dublin Horse Show. A filly Gurraun My Way foaled in 1999 by Grosvenor Lad won fifteen first prizes and six championships as a foal. Shown twice as a yearling she won two first prizes and a championship at Galway Show. At her inspection she passed with a total of 157 marks out of 165.

Bundrameen Lass

Bundrameen Lass (10016) 1976 grey by Ben Purple (580) out of Bundrameen Dolly (8333) by Glen of Aherlow (484) Bred by Timothy Crowley, Co Cork owned by James Crowley. A Greenvale champion. She bred eight foals between 1979 and 1983

Cappacurry Belle

Cappacurry Belle (11941) 1995 Bay by Corran Ginger (812) out of Ireland's Isle (11256) by Ireland's Pride (705) out of Black Magic (AID) by Vivadari (TB) Bred by Deirdre Robinson, Co Laois. Owned by Dawn Feerick, Co Mayo. Cappacurry Belle won many first prizes in showing classes as well as two championships. She was second in the All Ireland two year old filly championship in 1992.

Carrick Rose Blossom

Carrick Rose Blossom (12107) 1993 chesnut by Copper King (742) out of Wild Rosie (11035) by Mountain View (638) out of Rose Lahinch (AID) by Lahinch (558) Premier Brood mare. Bred by Leonard Lucas, Co Donegal. Owned by Viona Coulter, Co Tyrone.

Coppery Coin

Coppery Coin (11650) 1984 chesnut by Gold Coin (628) out of Lady Glenside (9664) by Glenside (563) out of Kelly (ISH) Bred by Patrick O'Riordan, Co Cork Owned by Vivienne Bradley, Co Laois. Bred six foals.

Doonmore Damsel

Doonmore Damsel (7835) 1968 grey by Atlantic Boy (527) out of Willow Maid bred by Christy Haugh, Co Clare and owned by Michael Griffin Co Clare. A Greenvale champion. She bred eleven foals between 1978 and 1992.

Derrynagarra Clorin

Derrynagarra Clorin (12007) by Crosstown Dancer out of Banks Fee Annabel owned and bred by Helen Kelly, won the young mare class at the national breed show in 2000 and 2001. Reserve champion mare National Breed Show 2000. She was a winner at Dublin Horse show in 2000. Her foal by

Blue Rajah was a winner at Dublin Horse Show 2001

Enniskeane Flash

Enniskeane Flash (11935) by Mountain Pearl (828) out of Enniskeane Primrose (11074), by Ginger Dick (643) bred by Billy Cotter and owned by John Cotter. Dam line pedigree goes back to Enniskeane Countess. Champion mare at Dublin 2001, champion national show 2000, all Ireland champion 2000.

Fast Woman

Fast Woman (10289) 1978 grey by Slievenamon (682) out of Hard and Fast (6254) by Kantogher Pride (455). Bred by Charles Lawless, Co Tipperary, owned by Michael Duggan Walshe, Co Tipperary. See chapter Special Mares.

Glen Heste Duchess

Glen Heste Duchess (11694) 1993 roan by Uibh Fhaili '81 (764) out of Glen Heste Princess by Legaun Prince (660). Quality Brood Mare. Bred and owned by Noel C Hamilton, Co Wicklow

Hard Silver

Hard Silver (10706) by Silver Hunter (681)1983 grey owned by Gordon and Vivienne Bradley, Stradbally, Co Laois and bred by Sean Walshe, Knockboy Stud, Thurles, Co Tipperary. Winner of the 1992 Slieve Bloom Championship and Leitrim Breeders Championship. Bred eight foals 1988 to 1997.

Lady in Red

Lady in Red by Grosvenor Lad out of Ginger Grace (11893) by Ginger Dick (643) out of Bulkane Lass (11861) by Grey Macha (746) bred by Eddie Murphy, Co Mayo Champion Young

Irish Draught Horse and National Show Supreme Champion 2000.

Levaghy Blue

Levaghy Blue (11854) 1992 grey by Blue Rajah (759) out of Hillcrest Grey Dawn (10749) by Knocknagow (600) Quality Broodmare. Bred by Loughrey College of Agriculture, Co Tyrone. Owner Robert Davis, Co Donegal.

Lismeen Countess

Lismeen Countess (10813) 1986 grey by Grey Macha (746) out of Coolgreen Countess (10457) by Slievenamon (682) Bred by Patrick Gleeson, Co Limerick and owned by Luke Smith, Co Cavan

Lismeen Diamond

Lismeen Diamond (11573) 1992 grey by Diamond Lad (695) out of Lismeen Countess (10813) by Grey Macha (746) out of Coolgreen Countess (10457) by Slievenamon (682) Bred and owned by Luke Smith, Co Cavan.

Lucille 3

Lucille 3 (10237) 1977 grey by King of Diamonds (547) out of Hard and Fast (6254) by Kantogher Pride (455). Bred by Charles Lawless, Tipperary and owned by Ronnie McCombe. Lucille bred three foals all fillies including showjumper Sandycove by Bright Will. Lucille won classes throughout Ireland and was champion in Dublin

Madden Lady

Madden Lady (10925) 1987 chesnut by Powerswood Purple (737) out of Mary Jane 3 (10335) by Atlantic Boy (527). Bred by John Madden, Co Galway, and owned by James Hoare, Co Kildare. Bred eight foals to 1999. A Quality Brood Mare.

James Hoare purchased Madden Lady as a foal in 1987. She won the first Irish Shows Association filly championship as a yearling and the following year won the two year old championship. He first foal was the colt Kilmadden Gold by Kildalton Gold who was registered as a stallion in England. Shje was sent to KKildalton Gold and Glenagyle Rebel and in 2002 was in foal to Crosstown Dancer. All her progeny were successful and she was only barren once. The Hoares have retained fillies by Kildalton Gold and Glenagyle Rebel for breeding.

Millhollow Queen

Millhollow Queen (12136)1997 roan by Annaghdown Star (791) out of Tempting Touch (11422) by Duleek Hero (760) out of May Queen 2 (9248) by Blue Peter (536) Bred by Moira McKenna, Co Down owned by Dawn Feerick, Co Mayo. Millhollow Queen was All Ireland Young Horse Champion at the Irish Draught Nationl Show at Mallow in 1999 and was reserve champion in Dublin as a three year old in 2000. She has won many championships all over Ireland.

My Hilltop Lady

My Hilltop Lady (11554) 1992 grey by Western Light (772) out of April Storm (10419) by Blue Peter (536) out of Silver Dawn 2 (10231) Premium Brood mare Bred by N and C Moore, Co Antrim owned by Diane Cameron, Co Derry. Winner of All Ireland clases as yearling and two year old, Limerick Lady championship and 1996 winner at Dublin and Blmoral. Reserve champion Broodmare national Irish Draught show 1997.

Nancy Steele

Nancy Steele (11834) by Holycross (763) out of Whitechurch Sal (AID) by Golden Warrior (752)1994 grey.

Bred by Patrick Hegarty Co Cork and owned by Suzanne Finlay, Co Tyrone. Supreme champion mare at national show 2001.

Pink Carnation

Pink Carnation (10516) by Goleen (584) out of White Carnation (5798) by Merrion (447 out of Coronation (4690) Bred and owned by Patrick Duane, Co Galway. Winner of the first Greenvale Championship in 1977. Pink Carnation bred ten foals from 1974 to 1987 including Gort Boy, English registered stallion by Grey Macha.

Pride of Monaghan

Pride of Monaghan (12140) 1997 chesnut by Kildalton Son (823) out of No Goal (115140 By Uibh Fhailli '81 (764) out of Corker Lass (10664) by Mountain View (638) Bred by David Curley, Co Galway out of No Goal and purchased by Vincent Burns, Co Monaghan, after a win at Corrundulla Show in Co Galway. She won the two year old Irish Draught class at Castlewellan Show and went on to take the Irish Draught Youngstock Championship. She then captured the Irish Draught National 2 year old filly championship final at Limerick Show. She won the three year old filly class at the Irish Draught National Show at Necarne in 2000. Her first foal was a colt by Annaghdown Star.

Roma Blue Wind

Roma Blue Wind (12071) by Blue Henry (744) out of Kiltowra Glee (8967) Bred by Mary Flynn Co Westmeath. Owned by Moira McKenna, Co Down.

Roma Silver Pearl

Roma Silver Pearl (11890) 1990 grey by Silver Jasper (712) out of Roma Blue Wind (12071) by Blue Henry (744) Bred and owned by Moira McKenna, Co Down Winner

Dublin Horse Show 2000.

Seafin Lady

Seafin Lady (10309) 1978 chesnut by Slievenamon (682) out of Dana's Pride (7715) by Milestone (498). Bred by William Bourke, Co Tipperary. Owners John and Sharon Alexander, Cullbackey, Co Antrim. Seafin Lady bred eight foals including The Blue Lady 1989 by Blue Rajah (759) winner of fifteen brood mare championships including Irish Draught mare champion and breeders champion Dublin Horse show 1996. Seafin Lady was three times Dublin Horse Show Irish Draught champion and twice national champion mare.

Skymist

Skymist (10637) 1983 grey by Skylark (627) out of Grange Mist (10333) by Silver Hunter (681) bred by John O'Shea and owned by Patrick F Greenan, Co Down.

The Blue Lady

The Blue Lady by Blue Rajah (759) out of Seafin Lady (10309) By Slievenamon (682) out of Dana's Pride (7715) by Milestone (498) bred by John Alexander, Co Antrim. The Blue Lady won several championships and is a full brother to the stallion Touch of the Blues.

Urney Pride

Urney Pride (11540) 1991 grey roan by Grey Macha (746) out of Lavally Pride AID by Atlantic Boy (527) out of Hilshanny (ISH) by Chairlift (TB) Premier Brood mare. Bred by Joseph Stanford, Co Galway, owned by Sean Colhoun, Co Tyrone. Urney Pride won a series of championships throughout Ireland including Best Young Irish Draught mare at Saintfield in 1996, Supreme Championship at Newry 1996, champion mare at Virginia 1996 and Champion Brood mare at

Finn Valley. Other wins were at Enniscrone, Tydavnet, Ballyshannon, Donegal Town, Ballina, Armagh, Westport, Bonagee. She won at Dublin Horse Show in 1995 and was the Northern Ireland Irish Draught champion mare of the year in 1995. She won some 60 other first prizes at various shows. Her foals include Florida Lady by Florida Sun 1996, supreme champion Finn Valley 1998 and first prize winner at other shows; Blue Moon by Blue Rajah 1997 winner at Dublin Horse Show and at six other venues. Northern Ireland Irish Draught Horse Society Foal of the Year 1997; Blue Saphire by Blue Rajah 1999, winner at Dublin Horse Show and five firsts as yearling; High Alert by Art Bright 2000, first at Necarne as foal and winner of eight firsts as yearling.

Warren Lass

Warren Lass (8719) 1971 grey by Brandon Hill (517) out of Warren Wonder (7195) by Tomboy. Bred by Timothy Sullivan, Co Laois. Owned by Michael Murphy Wexford. Warren Lass won the Greenvale Championship in 1982. Warren Lass bred ten foals between 1976 and 1985 including the stallion Sillot Hill (735) by Slievenamon (682)

Whippy

Whippy (10426) 1981 grey by Blue Peter (536) out of Softee (10243) by Skylark (627). See chapter Special Mares.

Irish Draughts in Britain

The Irish Draught Horse Society in Britain mirrors its counterpart society in Ireland in many ways, both in occasional acrimonious internal disputes and the apparently indominitable zeal of its hard core of committed members. Founded in 1979, the British organisation went through through a constitutional change in 2000 to convert it to a guarantee company with charitable status and has finally conformed to the Irish regulations on registration and closing its studbook. The society has its origins in a letter written to *Horse and Hound* by Mrs Dorothy Holmes of Norfolk asking for people to contact here and set up a breed society. Seventeen replied. The new organisation opened for business with two mares on its books.

The studbook closed on January 1, 2001 and part bred fillies are no longer eligible for the breed register divisions RID, AID (Appendix) or SID (Supplementary). The British organisations registration system is quite complex compared to the relatively straight foward Irish process. The Society has A, B, C and D Grades as well as G2 and G3 sections for animals that fail the inspection but pass the vet and for those that fail the vet. There are G2 and G3 grades in the Sport Horse register as well.

Part breds, previously excluded from the main studbook, are provided for by the Sport Horse Register and do not have to be inspected. The minimum proportion of ID blood required for the Sport Horse Register is 25%. Owners of already graded AID and SID mares stay on the register and their female progeny by an RID stallion are eligible for inspection and grading. The studbook was in fact closed to mares without papers some years ago, but until then mares arriving from Ireland without papers were eligible for SID or AID if they were true to type.

AID and SID mares are gradually being phased out to promote the purity of the breed. RID registration is confined to fillies out of RID and existing AID mares are eligible for full status. Fillies from existing SID mares by an RID stallion are eligible for AID.

The registration changes were forced on the British society by the Ministry for Agriculture (now the Department of Environment, Food and Rural Affairs) there which has insisted on the implementation of the Irish regime in the UK and would not recognise the British society until these changes had been introduced. One of the features of the change is that stallions can no longer be re-inspected for health defects. Ministry approval is essential for the society in Britain. Its former chairman Maggie Spreckley has made the point that without it breed stock there would be devalued and would not even be able to call themselves Irish Draughts.

Not all Irish Draught supporters in Britain agree with the changes. Some of them in fact view them as a step backwards. They were not, however, open for debate. Under EU legislation, to obtain recognition studbooks must be approved by the national breeding authority (the Departments of Agriculture of Ireland and Britain) to comply with EU directives. British breeders view the blocking of the system allowing for reinspection of stallions at six and nine years of age as a retrograde step. It has also had financial implications for the British society.

Fifty RID stallions stood in Britain for the 2001 season plus a further ten Sport Horse sires. One of the features of the breeding scene generally there for the past few years has been a decline in society memberships and registrations. The IDHS (GB) launched a drive for members and recruited around 100 newcomers and there are now around 900. The downward trend in coverings and registered foals which has been evident over the past five or six years unfortunately continues. In 1994 the number of coverings was 872. The foal registration figure was 577. Coverings fell by around 100 in 1995 with just under 500 foals registered. In 1998 the number of coverings was 500 and the number of registered foals 314.

These figures include foals from all types of mares within the society's registration system as well as thoroughbreds, thoroughbred crosses and other breeds. The majority of mares were covered by breed sires with just over 40 by Sport Horse sires. However only 24% were fully registered RID mares. Nearly sixty per cent of the mares covered were thoroughbred or thoroughbred crosses. The pure bred foal total in 1998 was 114.

Most Popular Stallions

On the basis of recorded coverings the most popular sire in Britain in 1999 was **Roma Diamond Skip** who attracted 45 mares, followed by Darcy Dancer 33 and Banks Fee Daniel 23. Of the remaining stallions only 13 attracted more than 1 0 mares. The rest were in single figures.

The 1992 16.3 hh liver chesnut Roma Diamond Skip, a son of Shauna's Diamond made a successful foray to Dublin Horse Show in 1996 when he took the blue ribbon in the Irish Draught stallion class. He stands in Hertfordshire with Mrs Jane Manning who bought him from Devon based Robin Cook who had been a importer of stallions from Ireland for a number of years. Roma's sire Shauna's Diamond (by Diamonds are Trumps) who also stands in the UK was bred from Michael Gavin's champion mare Shauna. Shauna's Diamond showjumped in Britain and collected £500 in BSJA winnings He was approved in Ireland in 1987 but went to the UK almost immediately.

Darcy Dancer is a 1980 16.3 hh son of Pride of Shaunlara. He stands near York with Mr and Mrs S.W. Knowles. His dam is Silver Queen by Blue Peter. He has built a reputation for producing performance progeny.

The bay **Banks Fee Daniel** is a 16.3 hh 1990 son of Skippy. He has an older full brother sire Banks Fee Jester. They were bred from a mare called Barna Lucy by Station Master. Banks Fee Daniel certainly rates as one of the more successful of the younger stallions. He has jumped under BSJA rules for two seasons and has produced a string of showring successes both in Britain and the USA. He has won the society's fertilty award on several occasions. He now stands in the USA.

The Irish Draught has made a fairly substantial input to performance in the UK over the years. There are 2,742 competition horses on the British database which have Irish Draught ancestry and which compete in the three disciplines. Of these 63.8% are by RID sires and 17.2% are by Irish Sport Horse sires. A very substantial per centage of the dams, 78.6% have no pedigree details, but 16.4% are ID crosses.

Competition Horses

Fifty Irish Draught sires based in Ireland and Britain have been identified by Mary McGowan, who maintains a performance data base for the society, as having six or more progeny competing successfully under the rules of the three major equestrian societies in Britain, showjumping, eventing, and dressage. These identified progeny are all fifty per cent Irish Draught.

The list obviously includes the deceased star performance sires, Clover Hill and King of Diamonds, fourteen of the fifty leading sires are in fact dead, but there are nonetheless a sufficient number of Irish based sires still contributing to the UK performance picture. Clover Hill has 157 competing progeny with 118 in showjumping, forty eventing and 18 dressage. Diamond Lad is in second place with 42 identified competing progeny, most of these in showjumping. Prospect Pride and Kildalton Gold have 31 each, while Kildalton King is just one slot behind them. Again these are jumpers. British based sires such as Embla George and Enniskeane Prince have produced dressage horses as well as showjumpers.

An Irish Draught stallion, the fourteen year old **Amber Glen**, by Merrygold owned by J. D. Tyndall has reached Grade A under BSJA rules. Under British rules horses must have won £1800 to become Grade A. He joins the ID Sport Horse Stallion, Millbrook Esquire by Enniskeane Prince owned by two ladies Louise Morton and Lynne Bevan who is also Grade A. Amber Glen was bred by the British society's vice president Prof K Hinkley.

Amber Glen began his career as a yearling owned by Robin and Margaret Cook at Roma Stud. He won the yearling class and became Supreme champion at the National Breed Show in 1988. He was a winner again the following year and as a three year old was bought by Desmond Tyndall. In 2000 he was the first Irish Draught stallion to reach Grade A in Britain. He was awarded the newly created Silver status for stallions by the

BSJA. He will get gold if he gets a place on an international British team. Amber Glen has a sport horse stallion son Ringwood Four Square 1996 chesnut owned by Mrs D Mason, Billerclay, Essex.

Irish Draught pedigrees have made their own special contribution to British eventing. One successful performer is Daisy Dick's Headley Bravo by Skippy. Skippy has had another successful representative with Alfred of Church Farm. Another achiever was Camilla Hall's Taylor Made by Touchstone. There are well over 200 competing eventers by Irish Draught sires in Britain.

The Irish Draught Horse Society GB has an annual performance award scheme whereby competitiors gain points from competitions in which they were prizewinners. Disciplines covered are the ridden categories showjumping, dresage, horse trials, side saddle plus driving. The 2001 winner was Outstanding with 5155 points owned by Mrs Helen Trivett. Outstanding by Silver Skip was bred in Co Donegal by Michael Gibbons.

One of the important breed promotion incentives operated by the society is the annual award of Hornby Trust Premiums to top quality mares of all grades. The Premiums are awarded at the mare inspections each year. The mares must score a minimum of 150 points at the inspection. This is the equivalent of the mark required for a colt to be approved as a stallion. When inspected mares must have a foal at foot by an RID stallion although the foal is not taken into account in the assessment. The thinking is that a mare should not be penalised because a current foal is not up to the standard of those bred previously. At least a dozen premiums are awarded each year. The object of the premium scheme is to encourage people with top class mares to breed, purebred foals. A new rule was introduced in 2001. After being awarded her third Hornby Premium a mare will be given the title of Select Hornby Premium Mare which she will hold for life. She may not be brought forward for assessment again but from that point onwards, all her purebred foals will be registered free of charge.

There is an annual fertility award for stallions which must cover a minimum of fifteen mares. The trophy was given to the society by Robin and Margaret Cook. A Performance Award is made each year.The Society stages an annual breed show and there are fourteen other major shows throughout the UK where Irish Draught classes are staged.

Obviously the foundation stock for the Irish Draughts in Britain were exported from Ireland. The dominant Irish families exerted a strong influence. The British breeders produced their own stallions from their imported sires and built up bloodlines whose current sires are little known in Ireland.

King of Diamonds

As might be expected King of Diamonds and Pride of Shaunlara exerted a strong influence. **Shauna's Diamond**, a showjumping son of Diamonds are Trumps from Michael Gavin's good mare Shauna, established a reputation as a performance sire and has stallion sons, **Roma Diamond Skip** and **Pary's Patricks Day** on the British stallion register. Shauna's Diamond stands with FK Turnock, Peterhead. Roma Diamond Skip is with Mrs J Manning in Herefordshire, and Pary's Patricks Day is with the Farrells, Anglesey. Creggan Diamond produced **Alice's Diamond Slipper**. who stands with Mrs J Shaw in Devon. Flagmount Boy, the performance tested son of King of Diamonds sent over the 1978 **Purple Boy** out of the Ben Purple mare Curragh Heather. Curragh Heather owned by Donal McCarthy, Co Cork bred ten foals from 1974 to 1990. Purple Boy is with D Croft in Buckinghamshire. **Riverbank** foaled in 1981 by Kintara out of Carrigbawn Colleen is another of King of Diamonds descendant stallions in Britain. He stands in Mansfield with Miss G Smith.

Touch of Pride by Milestone Pride 1995 liver chesnut is a grandson of King of Diamonds out of Corlea Tessie. He carries King of Diamonds on both sides. Corlea Tessie was a daughter of Flagmount Boy while Milestone Pride was a son of Ireland's Pride. The Milestone influence is on the dam side of his sire. He stands with Norman Evans in Carmarthenshire, Wales. Touch of Pride is 16.3 hh with nine and three quarter inches of bone. He was bred by Mr and Mrs Cartwright in Worcestershire. Norman Evans says he is an excellent mover and has a very nice temperament. He is the only registered Irish Draught stallion by Milestone Pride, also owned by Norman Evans, who was exported from Ireland in 1984 as a two year old. He was bred by E. Martin, Templemore, Co Tipperary. His dam Cluan Mor was a well known show mare in the 1970s.

Glenbrae (776) 1984 by Parnell (642) who stands with Hazel Morris in Wales is a daughter of the Flagmount Diamond mare Lady Glen (10384).

Wyzer Diamond, a 1990 son of Glidawn Diamond by King of Diamonds out of the Grove Hero mare Gesagh Lass stands with Sam Thompson at Broombrae Farm, Kilmarnock in Scotland. Glidawn Diamond was a daughter of Kildalton Countess by Ben Purple (See chapter Special Mares). He was bred by Mr and Mrs Denis Horgan. Sam Thompson junior showjumped Wyzer

Diamond for a time but due to his career was unable to continue with showjumping. Wyzer Diamond had four year olds in 2001. Some of his stock have done well in showing classes, particularly a colt foal called Diamond Wise Guy. His owner describes Wyzer Diamond as a big (16.2hh) modern Irish Draught stallion bred from a very good jumping line, quick in his action and light on his feet. He was brought over from Ireland by the Thompsons in 1995.

Errigal the sire of King of Diamonds continues his influence with the 1984 liver chesnut son of Slyguff Hero, King of Diamonds' full brother, **Knockboy Hero** out of Cummer Queen by Milestone. He measures 16.1hh and has nine and three quarter inches of bone and stands with Mrs Alison Ives, of Balinmore Stud Driffield, East Yorks. Knockboy Hero was bred by Philip Maher, Thurles. Slyguff Hero stood with Sean Walshe, Thurles. Cummer Queen is a daughter of Milestone. Mrs Ives says that Knockboy Hero has a very laid back approach to life and is a very kind gentle horse. His stock are excellent performers. He has showjumping progeny and has produced county show winners, show hunters and registered Irish Draught mares. Some of his purebred stock have ben exported to Canada. He is ridden at home and has hunted.

Tobias Corbett 1986 chesnut son of Slyguff Hero out of Run Away stands with G. Veal at Umberleigh in Devon.

Pride of Shaunlara

Pride of Shaunlara has exercised a strong influence through his son grey son **Finbarr** foaled in 1976. Finbarr has produced three stallion son on the British Register. Finbarr a smaller compact Irish Draught was foaled in 1976. He stands with Mark Fitton at N ew Hill Farm Stud, Worsley,

Manchester. HIs dam was Gloun Rover by Gortlee **Foxglen Finn** is a 1992 chesnut out of Sally standing with Mrs A Beattie, Strathclyde in Scotland. **Foxglen Himself** a 1991 full brother to Foxglen Finn stood with Mrs Caroline Saynor near Wakefield. He is now in the USA. Finbarr's third son is **Walton's Golden Fox** a 1997 chesnut out of Kallisto Countess standing with Mrs L. Hunt, Royston, Herts.

Enniskeane Countess exported two important sons to England, **Enniskeane Pride** foaled in 1976 and **Enniskeane Prince** foaled in 1979. Enniskeane Pride stands with Mrs S. Goodlad, Tuxford Notts and Enniskeane Prince is in Staffordshire with Duco Van Joolan and Louise Morton, the Lingbourne Stud. Enniskeane Prince has two sport horse stallion sons, the Grade A Millbrook Esquire, 1988 bay owned by Miss Morton and Miss Lynne Bevan and Knightly Park, brown 1992 owned by Miss Louise Morton.

Enniskeane Prince foaled in 1979 and bred by Billy Cotter, is the only registered Irish Draught sire to appear on both the British Dressage and the BSJA Top Twenty Living Sires. He was imported to Britain as a two year old. Enniskeane Prince is described as having a wonderful temperament and is a good free mover which he passes on to his progeny. He has been an important influence on the Irish Draught in Britain, purebred and halfbred.

Millbrook Esquire is an exceptionally talented stallion and has achieved numerous successes with part owner Lynne Bevan and is a Grade A showjumper and registered Irish Draught Sport Horse sire. A bay foaled in 1988 he stands 16.1hh. His dam was the thoroughbred Horton Foxy Gamble by Crespino out of Sara Dane by Ozymandias, an intermediate event mare. She was the dam of the intermediate FEI eventer

Foxtone by Milestone Pride. Millbrook Esquire is life approved as an RID sporthorse and is also approved by the Anglo European Studbook.

The 1992 RID sport horse stallion **Knightly Park**, also owned by the Lingbourne Stud is a versatile performer and has competed in ridden, dressage, working hunter and BSJA competitions. He was bred by S Barnes from a thoroughbred mare Sophisticated Lady.

Gort Boy by Grey Macha is a great grand son of Pride of Shaunlara. He was bred from the first winner of the Greenvale Mare Championship, Pink Carnation owned by Patrick Duane. A 1984 grey, Gort Boy stands with J. Durant, Doncaster. He has a stallion son on the British register, the 1991 grey **Kerryoak Captain** out of Taicyd Alice who stands with Mrs and Mrs Turrell in Carmarthen.

O'Sullivan by Pride of Toames is a grandson of Pride of Shaunlara. His dam was the show mare Ballybane Grace (7846) by Aughadown (565). Ballybane Grace owned by Bernard Stanford, of Gort, also bred his stallion Grey Macha by Pride of Toames. O'Sullivan has two stallion sons on the British register. **Amber Legend** a 1989 16.3 hh grey with ten inches of bone is out of Crofters Diamond and stands with John and Sally Fox Fox, Providence House, Alkborough, Scunthorpe. Crofters Diamond is a daughter of Kintara who of course was by King of Diamonds. Crofters Diamond and her dam Crofters Golden Heather by Ben Purple are champion Irish Draught and Hornby Premium mares and have produced showring winners. Amber Legend was himself successfully shown in hand and has BSJA winnings in a few outings although he has been mainly concentrating on stud duties for the past few years. His successes include first at the Royal Show, and the Irish Draught Breed Show and first and reserve champion at Whitchurch show. He has been awarded the Ben Purple colt subsidy. He has showring winners.

Baracaberry Orbit a 1992 grey out of Beeston Elver stands with Mrs J Miller of Bridlington, East Yorkshire. Baracaberry Orbit competes in all disciplines including long distance riding and has been hunted. He has won in dressage, hunter trials and showjumping and was first in his class at the breed show 2000.

Ben Purple

Connaught Grey is a 1990 grey son of Powerswood Purple and grandson of Ben Purple out of Airport Rose. He stands with John and Kay Chapman in Derbyshire. He was bred in Ireland by Christy Grealish and won two championships as a foal. He was shown a bit by the Chapmans as a youngster winning a second at the Great Yorkshire show. He performed in dressage and showjumping and won £90 in 2001. Kay Chapman says he is extremely careful over a fence, very rarely knocking anything down. His technique and care over a fence impressed the judges at the Sport Horse Breeding (GB) inspections and he pased as Grade 1. Graham Fletcher complimented his owners on his technique and attitude in the jumping phase. Connaught Grey is hunted regularly with the High Peak Harriers. Kay Chapman says he is a true gentleman and extremely reliable hunter. As an indication of his good manners and temperament she cites an occasion when she was short of time for exercising an d had to take him out with a mare. She rode the stallion and took the mare in hand and although he thought this was very exciting managed to contain himself! This time saving method became a regular thing.

Coosheen Ballymurphy 1992 bay is by Torspark Benedict,

a son of Ben Purple, out of Coosheen Girl. He stands with Mrs Gaynor Mitchell at Ormskirk, Lancs. Coosheen Girl was a mare bought at a time when the Mitchell's daughter was coming out of ponies. She was in the hands of a dealer but had been bought from her previous owner in Co Clare. She had been fully registered and approved as an RID mare. They didn't know whether she was broken but they put a saddle and bridle on and she rode well if a little green. Later they were to discover that she had in fact never been broken.

Coosheen Girl is an exceptionally well made mare, bay 15.3 hh, by Clonmore Boy out of an unknown mare. She was always well placed at county level in Hunter brood mare classes and her foals/young stock did very well. She proved to have a first class jump and won a competition as a foal was being weaned after a riding break of eighteen months. She jumped four clear rounds to take the red rosette. She only had two pure bred colts and both were graded as stallions. Coosheen Liam is now in Australia after standing many years with Archie Smith-Maxwell at Upton on Severn. Coosheen Ballymurphy has inherited his dam's conformation and temperament. He is regularly ridden by by a fifteen year old girl. Mrs Mitchell says that she was fortunate to get the Clonmore Boy line as the breeding has always been consistent. She quotes Major Tim Hellyer as saying that a daughter of Coosheen Girl had near perfect conformation. In 2001 Coosheen Girl was 27 years of age.

Coosheen Ballymurphy has produced foals from thoroughbreds which finished with 9.5" bone. Mrs Mitchell is sure that this comes from the fact that he is pure ID with no thoroughbred influence. Although he produces bone and substance he has absolutely no feather and never has to have his heels clipped out. Mrs Mitchell comments that the sport horses are the money earners in the long term but they will not be there if the traditional draught is lost. She says that she is often told that temperaments never let down horses from this line in competition.

Donovan (859) carries Ben Purple on his dam side as the sire of Night Nurse 2. His son **Sir Lancelot** 1997 grey out of Balmoral stands at Shadwell Stud near Leeds. Donovan now stands in Ireland with Lawrence Flood in Co Kildare.

Snowford Benson 1985 chesnut out of Harepark Pink. He stands with Mrs S Bullock, Easingwold, York.

Laughton

Attwood Black Laughton (854) is a brown 1985 son of Ballinrobe Boy (703) by Ginger Dick, a son of Bell Laughton. Hisdam was Lydican Madam (10491) by Atlantic Boy (527), a son of the important sire Tara out of Lydican Daisy (7380) by Carrigfadda (535) He was bred by John Fahy and is owned by Caroline Saynor, Wakefield, West Yorks. He was approved in the UK in 1990. An influential brood mare sire, Attwood Black Laughton has produced show ring winners and competition horses. His progeny have been exported to the United States and back to Ireland. His owner Caroline Saynor says that he is a super horse and that she is very honoured to have owned him. She makes the point that he is a total outcross and so has a great deal to offer the purebred breeder of today. in 2001 his dam Lydicam Madam was alive and breeding in Galway.

Ballyknowe Prince

Ballyknowe Prince 1985 grey by Ballynoe Lad out of Grey Sovereign has been producing jumpers although he has not competed himself. His owner rides him at home. He stands with

Anne Beattie at Knowehead Farm, Harthill, Strathclyde. One of his progeny is Loughrea Gold who has won numerous working hunter championships and has competed at Gleneagles and Malvern and taken part in team events. Two more of his progeny have competed in the Newcomers at the Horse of the year Show. His dam Grey Sovereign by Dickie (577) was supreme champion at nineteen years of age at the Northern Irish Draught Show in 1993. He goes back to Young JP number 12 in the original Irish Draught Horse Book. He carries Kildare on his sire side and Galty Boy in the dam sire line.

Clonfert

Clonfert (694) has two representatives, the 1987 chesnut **Roma Atlantic Moonshine** out of Atlantic Beauty owned by Ann Adams Williams in Wales and **Snowford Pinkston** 1983 chesnut out of Harepark Pink owned by Hazel Morris of Ceredigion, Wales who also stands Glenbrae. Clonfert by Bawnlahan (585), out of Cousin Rachel (6053) by Blarney Castle (409) was a widely regarded stallion and stood with Vincent Faughnan in Leitrim before being exported to England. He was brought back to Ireland by David Cosby, a former chairman of the Irish Draught Horse Society in Britain.

Roma Atlantic Moonshine was bought as a yearling in summer 1988 and approved as a stallion in February 1990. He was broken and used for rounding up sheep and Welsh Black cattle with occasional cross country rides. His dam Atlantic Beauty by Atlantic Boy was a champion foal at Millstreet and qualfied there again as a three year old. She produced Moonshine in the same year shortly after arriving at the Roma Stud. She won many championships when owned by Roma Stud. She is the dam of the RID stallion Carhill Flight by Silver Jasper. Moonshine's first foal was Roma Atlantic Blue out of the championship mare Roma Blue Wind. Blue was a showring winner and show jumped as well. His second foal was Oldhouse High Moon a winner of many cob classes who was third at Wembley in 1996. Other foals including Oldhouse Kitty Moon, novice winner at Monmouth trials in 2000, have been successful in horse trials. Oldhouse Midnight Moon was purchased by Avon and Somerset police. Ann Adams Williams says that her interest in the Irish Draught began when she saw a picture of Merrion being shown at Dublin Horse Show in 1967.

Snowford Pinkston was foaled in 1983 and bred by Pam Symonds. He was approved in 1998 as a fifteen year old never having been presented before. Consequently some of his progeny are registered HIS. He has bred seventeen colts and fourteen fillies for Hazel Morris out of a range of mares. These are mostly Irish Draught crosses but she has a colt by an RID mare, Blithedale Lady foaled 2001. Hazel Morris says that his progeny are all very versatile and all possess his outstanding super temperament. He is ridden bareback with a head collar by Hazel Morris's seven year old grand-daughter although he has never been broken. Pinkston descends from Comet, number one, in the Irish Draught studbook, as does her other stallion Glenbrae. His dam Harepark Pink is the dam of four stallions, the important Snowford Stoker, Snowford Benson and Snowford O'Donnell who was exported. Pinkston runs out with his mares and foals. His mares have included pacers, Arabs, thoroughbreds, cobs and draught mares, other than those owned by Hazel Morris. Breeders have said that his progeny jump and have competed in long distance and dressage.

Colman

Colman (612) by Kilcolman (538) who traces back in the sire line to Tara (369) has two representatives on the stallion Register. His grandson **Beeston Lord Henry** by Coosheen Liam out of Pride of Shara Flynn by Pride of Shaunlara, 1993 bay stands with Mr and Mrs Chadwick, Elmhurst Farm, Thatcham, Newbury, Berks. He was bought as a three year old from his breeder Archie Smith Maxwell, then president of the Irish Draught Horse Society GB. He has been hunting and doing the local shows and cross country events. His progeny are making their mark in the showring. In 2001 Elmhurst Lady Henrietta won the Supreme Championship at the Irish Draught Breed Show at Three Counties Malvern. John Dunlop sent a mare who produced a chesnut filly Golden Virginia, who as a 2001 yearling won hunter yearling classes and was reserver champion at the Three Counties Show. The Chadwicks also stand Kenson's Mosaic a 1992 son of Silver Jasper out of the Grove Hero mare Brown Betty

Fintan Himself 1994 grey son of Uibh Fhailli '81 by Glenside is out of a Colman mare Colman's Gift. He stands with ER Sayce, West Glamorgan.

Kilmore Heather

Kilmore Heather by Poulgorm (546), a son of Abbeylara out of a Mountain Heather mare has two representatives standing as stallions. **Paddy's Pride** 1977 grey by Kilmore Heather out of Casting Vote stands with FK Turnock, Peterhead. Paddy's Pride produced the eventer Tritan Brigadier.

Hawklands Silver Prince 1992 grey son of Silver Jasper out of Knockany Princess and grandson of Kilmore Heather stands with Mrs Gail Payne, in Cornwall. He was inspected in 1996 and did some affiliated shows as a four year old He was ridden by Steve Payne at the National Irish Draught Show in 1999 and won the Ridden Hunter and Reserve Championship. He won the Skippy Too plate for the best performance stallion at the show in the following year. Gail Payne bought Knockany Princess in 1989 and kept her until 1993. She was in foal to Enniskeane Pride at the time of purchase. She was sold to Jane Manning in 1993 in foal to Rakish Paddy. She bred three foals while with the Paynes. One of these was Hawklands Silver Prince and another was Hawklands Princess Blue an RID mare which is used as a competition and riding horse by the family. She has showring winnings, has qualified for Wembley and Hickstead and has £271 BSJA winnings.

Rusheen Hero

Rusheen Hero (445) by Rossmore (171) has three representatives. Rusheen Lad has produced **Gortlea Ruler** 1986 brown out of Castleview who stands with Dr Hinckley and **Grove Warrior** 1986 bay grandson of Rusheen Hero by Grove Hero (629) out of Silver 13. He stands with Mrs A Schofield, Wickham Hants.

Rusheen Hero's grand son, **Kensons Aragorn** by Grove Ranger (765) 1988 brown out of Kilbarron Luck who goes back to the thoroughbred Lord Luck. He stands 16.2hh and has nine and three quarter inches of bone. He is owned by Gill Clothier and stands with Delerie Chambers, in Dorset. Rusheen Hero bred Georges Girl, the dam of Slievenamon and two stallion sons Baultic Hero and Rusheen Lad. Heather Honey, Paul Darragh's international showjumper was bred from a Rusheen Hero mare. Aragorn has competed in a wide variety of disciplines from team chasing to showing and dressage. He hunted for several seasons with the Blacmore and Sparkford Vale and also with a bloodhound pack. He won over £100 BSJA while based in Cornwall in 1998. He has since been competing in riding club dressasge and combined training and affiliated dressage. His young stock have performed well in the showring and in eventing at BHTA novice and intermediate level. He is the sire of a successful heavyweight show hunter, Tiny. Rusheen Hero appears in the paternal dam line of Minerva, dam of **Cork Arthur** by Heather Breeze (698) a son of Shandrum Prince (534). Cork Arthur on his sire side goes back to Young Arthur 2, number ten in the Irish Draught Horse Book and sire of Molly Grey dam of Kildare. He is owned by Dr KA Hinckley.

Skippy

Legaun Prince (660) by Milestone (498) had an important representative in Britain. This was Skippy (688) who produced the full brothers **Banks Fee Daniel** 1990 now in the USA and **Banks Fee Jester** 1984 out of Barna Lucy. She was by Stationmaster (633) by a thoroughbred horse Powerstation. Banks Fee Daniel stood with Mrs M Spreckley in Lincolnshire while Banks Fee Jester is with J. Goulding in Glostershire.

Skippy has two sport horse stallion sons, Haddon Challenger 1983. bay and Haddon Conquest 1985 chesnut, both owned by CJ Hewlett, of Marlborough, Wilts.

Legaun Prince has three other representatives, **Mountain Prince** owned by leading breeder Dr K Hinckley, of Derbyshire, and **Hillview Farm Milligan** a son of Rakish Paddy by Legaun Prince, owned by Mrs G Mitchell, Lancashire. Mountain Prince has a stallion son **Crofters Realm** 1985 chesnut out of Crofters Golden Heather owned by RA Pickard, Barham, Near Canterbury.

Timahoe Heather

Timahoe Heather by Glengoole Heather out of April Morn (4331) gave the British register two stallion sons. These are **Huntingfield Heathcliff** 1993 out of Blenheim Lady owned by Dr Hinckley and **Huntingfield Proud Tim** 1993 out of Proud Mary formerly owned by J. McCarthy of Huntingfield Proud Tim has been exported to Lucy Stephenson in the USA. Timahoe Heather was the stallion rescued by Robin and Margaret Cook. These two stallions were bred from him in his last season at the age of twenty

Touch of the Blues

Touch of the Blues, John and Sharon Alexander's son of Blue Rajah who was exported to the USA has four stallion sons on the British register. These are **Lady's Tralee Raj** 1991 grey out of Silver Lass who stands with Mark Fitton, Worsley; the black 1992 **On a High** out of Opium Poppy who stands with Miss G Smith at Mansfield; and the 1992 black **Ebony Hill** out of Embla Bow. His other stallion son was **Bealagh Blue.**

Lady's Tralee Raj produced the reserve supreme champion IDHS Breed Show 1999 and 2000. His owner describes him as a big horse that is light to ride, totally unflappable, extravagent, athletic and powerful. He whipped in for the North East Cheshire 1999.

Ebony Hill owned by PJ O'Gorman of Droitwich Worcs has twice won the Roma Stallion Fertility Trophy, in 1998 and 2000. He produced 16 foals from 19 coverings. He has successful showring progeny including the 2000 youngstock champion at the national breed show and in hand successes at county shows.

Touch of the Blues bred six stallion sons before being exported to the USA. Etherow Impasse has been exported to South Africa and Coalman's Touch has gone to New Zealand. Touch of the Blues was a son of Blue Rajah by Blue Peter. (See chapter

Stallions in North America).

Western Pride

Western Pride (704) a son of Lisheen (655) has two representatives on the register. The 1988 chesnut **Western Sun** by Western Pride out of Ard Lass stands with Caroline Saynor at Wakefield, West Yorkshire. **Lakeview Pride** (757) another son has **Roeview Pride** a 1989 grey out of Tullough Lassie 2 who stands with N Hargan, Dursley, Glos. Western Pride was a Grade A showjumper. His dam Ard Lass was placed on several occasions in the Kerrygold finals. Western Sun has BSJA winnings of over £400 and has since engaged in affiliated advance dressage. In November 2000 Western Sun was presented for grading with the Sport Horse of GB and was approved gaining scores of 8.5 in almost every section.

Rosie Hargan says of Roeview Pride that he has been a wonderful introduction to the Irish Draught breed having previously ridden thoroughbreds. He is, she says, a real treasure to her. She is privileged to have owned a horse with such a wonderful temperament and trusting nature. Roeview Pride stands 16.1hh and has nine inches of bone. He is described as a free oving athletic horse who has over eighty dressage points. He hunts and is a perfect gentleman at all times. He also competes in affiliated showjumping. The Hargans own his eldest son who competed at the Regional British Dressage championships in 2001 at novice and elementary level. He has over 50 points. Another son was second highest priced lot at the Festival of the Horse Sale at the Malverns in 2000.

Stallions in North America

Banks Fee Daniel

Banks Fee Daniel by Skippy out of Barna Lucy by Station Master was brought to the USA by his owner Maggie Sprekley who emigrated He is owned by Penmerryl Farm, Greenville VA where Maggie Spreckley is based. Barna Lucy's unnamed dam is believed to be by Errigal. Foaled in 1987 he is a bay standing 16.3 hh. Banks Fee Daniel was bred in Britain by Caroline Amphlet. Maggie Spreckley bought him as a foal when her dam went to visit Snowford Stoker. He won showjumping and cross country over the years, covered a lot of mares and has left good stock in Britain. He is Grade 1 NASTA and winner of the Progeny Group Award IDHS (GB) He was a seven times winner of the Roma Fertility Award, More than 36 of his progeny are competing in England and the US in dressage, showjumping and eventing.

A well conformed horse with very correct paces Banks Fee Daniel has a powerful big scopey jump. He has a kind easy disposition and exhibited great courage as a competition horse.

Cradilo

Cradilo by Kildalton Gold out of the Legaun Prince mare Brehan Lass was foaled in 1993 in Ireland. He is a chesnut standing 17.0hh He is owned by Laddbrook Farm 149 Bean Hill Road, Belmont, NH 03220. Laddbrook Farm is run by Cassandra and Jonathan Ladd.

Foxglen Himself

Foxglen Himself stands with Antony and Amy Phillips, Red Ridge Farm, 501 Swisher Road, Crimoira, VA 24431. A son of Finbarr by Pride of Shaunlara out of the Flagmount Boy mare Sally, he was foaled in 1991 in Wales. He is a grey standing 16.3 hh.

Glenlara

Glenlara (847) is a 1987 grandson of Pride of Shaunlara by Enniskeane Pride (717) a son of Enniskeane Countess, the dam of Kildalton Countess. Glenlara's dam is Night Nurse 2 (10054) by Ben Purple (580) He was approved in the UK in 1990 and returned to Ireland to stand with Dermot McCarthy at Twogneeves, Drimoleague, Co Cork. He was bred by P. McCarthy. He is owned by Oak Hill Farm, 18320 Yellow Schoolhouse Road, Roundhill VA 20141

Grange Augustus

Grange Augustus foaled in 1988 is a son of Enniskeane Prince out of Pilgrim's Gift. He is a grey and stands 16.2 hh. He stands with Keene Saxon, 18368 Eisenhower Rd, Leavenworth, KS 66048. His owner describes Grange Augustus as a gentle horse. There are several other stallions on the farm which is a working cattle and horse enterprise but Grange Augustus is the only Irish Draught in the area. He is used purely for breeding and does not compete, but is occasionally ridden out on the ranch. Gus, says his owner, is a good friend and a gentleman.

Hang on Johnny

Hang on Johnny is a son of Powerswood Purple foaled in 1988 and bred by John Madden. He was Approved in the UK in 1991 and is owned by Michael Lackman of Iowa. His dam was Mary Jane (10335) by Atlantic Boy out of a Rusheen Hero mare

Jane Eyre 3 (6598).

Happy Ending

Happy Ending was foaled in England in 1988. He is a son of Snowford Stoker out of Trinity by Merrygold. He was performance tested in England and awarded Grade 1 Elite. He is owned by Pennmerryl Farm, PO Box 402, Greenvale VA 24440. UP to the time of his performance test Happy Ending was the only Irish Draught stallion to have successfully completed the Nasta test at Grade 1 Elite. He gained 140 marks. His sire Snowford Stoker was a champion sire and replicates his sire's jumping ability. He has been a consistent winner of clases in both England and the USA. A dark bay with nine and a half inches of bone he stands 16.2hh

His accomplishments in the USA include winning the 1999 Breed show championship, the supreme performance championship and Jumping Championship in the same year. He was the sire of the best part bred foal 1998 and 1999. His BSJA winnings totalled £250. His dam Trinity has twice received the broodmare of the year award presented by the British Horse Database. She is the dam of Blue Rajah who stands with John and Sharyn Alexander in Ireland. Trinity goes back to Laughton on her sire side. Snowford Stoker was a son of Colman. He was bred by Jackie Ross. He was produced by Maggie Spreckley who inherited him as a foal.

Hello Paddy

Hello Paddy is a 1996 son of Rakish Paddy out of the Pride of Shaunlara mare Scaplire. He is a grey standing 16.1hh He is owned by Lance and Liesa Grundy, Rolly View, ALB TOC 2k0 Canada. He was bred by Sally Begg. He was sold to the USA as a two year old and bought by the Grundys after approval in 2000. He is breeding and working as a hunter/jumper.

Herrero

Herrero (843) is a 1993 son of Kildalton Gold (774)bred by Kildalton Countess and is a great grandson of Pride of Shaunlara on his dam side. She was Brehan's Pride (10797) by Pride of Toames (686) by Pride of Shaunlara. Her dam was Brehan Lass (10374) by Legaun Prince (660). Bred by Chantal Deon he is owned by Anne Dann, Florida.

Huntingfield Proud Tim

Huntingfield Proud Tim is a son of Timahoe Heather out of the Pride of Shaunlara mare Proud Mary. He is a chesnut standing 17.2hh. He is owned by Lucy Stephenson, Dandylion Farm, Stevensville, Montana.

It's the Luck of the Irish

It's the Luck of the Irish is a 1996 Maine USA bred son of Flagmount King out of the Glenagyle Rebel mare Maggie's Last, a daughter of Mrs Thatcher by Blue Peter. He is a grey standing 16.2 hh. He is owned by Diane Player, Playland Farm, 12924 Molasses Road, Union Bridge, Maryland 21791.

KEC Double Diamond

KEC Double Diamond (866) is a 1996 chesnut son of Glidawn Diamond (754) by King of Diamonds (547) out of Ballyard Katie (11786) by Creggan Diamond (755) out of Ballinorig Dolly and AID mare. Glidawn Diamond is a daughter of Kildalton Countess (10180). Creggan Diamond was a son of Diamond Lad (695) by King of Diamonds. He was bred by Michael Daly and produced and exported by William Kennedy. He is owned ny Jutta Heinsohn, Adsagona Farm.

Kilpeck Diamond Knight

Kilpeck Diamond Knight is a 1997 son of Roma Diamond Skip

out of the Slyguff Hero mare Knockany Princess. He was foaled in England. He is a chesnut standing 17.2hh and has ten inches of bone. He is owned by Chelsea McLeod, 120 Irving Young Road, RR2 Scotsburn, Pictou Co, Nova Scotia, BOK 1R0. Chelsea McCleod bought Kilkpeck Diamond Knight as a foal from his breeders Martin and Jane Manning of Kilpeck Stud in the UK. He was inspected and approved in Canada and was the first Irish Draught to be passed and stand there. His owner says that she couldn't be more pleased with him or the breed. She says that although a bit massive he is very light and responsive to ride. He is being trained for eventing with a strong dressage base. HIs first foal crop is due in 2002. His fertility has been good with all his mares being in foal even from shipped semen. "I really enjoy my boy," Chelsea McLeod says. "He has the greatest personality and is a real gentle giant with an incredible intelligence.

Macha Breeze

Macha Breeze foaled 1998 is a son of Grey Macha out of the Heather Breeze mare A Light Breeze. He is a grey standing 16.2hh. He is owned by Frank and Kitty Olivito, Abbeyleix Farm Sanford NC and stands with Dr Barbara Siegel, Stand and Deliver Farm, West End, NC. Macha Breeze was approved in North America. He was being broken to saddle in 2002 . Kitty Olivito was the founding chairwoman of IDHSNA and was the first judge of Irish Draughts in North America. She made three tours with the inspectors. Macha Breeze was bred by the late Tobias Corbett, Thurles, Co Tipperary. Macha Breeze's dam is a daughter of Heather Breeze, a relatively rare stallion line.

The same owners have a young stallion Moorpark Image by Moorpark Boy. This is also a rare line and the Olivitos hope to preserve this with the eventual approval of this 1999 bay. His dam was Rockbarton Beauty a daughter of Flagmount Boy and carries King of Diamonds blood.

Mountain Pearl

Mountain Pearl (828) is a 1989 bay son of Mountain View (638) by Glen Star (478) out of Grey Streaker (8722) by Bantry Pearl (525) a son of Abbeylara (476). He is owned by Petrie Jensen, Bloomington, Minnesota and stands at Fox Hollow Sport Horses. He was bred by A. Crowley in Co Cork and later owned by John McCarthy. He won a number of prizes as a youngster and was amongst the first draft in the newly introduced performance testing system in 1993. He stood with Gladys Nesbitt in Co Monaghan until his export to the USA late in 1997. He has 134 foals registered in Ireland. He has not competed in the USA but has been a success at stud. Two of his older offspring are competing in hunter and jumper competitions in the USA.

His purebred offspring are winning in the showring. Pearls for Diana out of Lady Di, was Purebred mare Champion in North America for two years as well as Youngstock Champion. Another Knockderry Pearl was Reserve Champion at the IDHSNA show. His most noted offspring in Ireland is Enniskeane Flash bred by Billy Cotter out of Enniskeane Primrose. She is the 2001 RDS champion and All Ireland champion in 1999 and 2000, the Aer Rianta champion 2000 and Supreme champion at the IDHS National show in 1999.

O'Leary's Irish Diamond

O'Leary's Irish Diamond (845) is a 1994 grey son of Glidawn Diamond (754) by King of Diamonds (547) out of Grey Curragong (10640) by the Conqueror (715) by Flagmount Boy (683) a son of King of Diamonds. He is owned by Jim Leary, Lamy, New Mexico and was bred by Anna Kennedy.

O'Leary's Irish Diamond scored the highest conformation points of his year at his inspection in 1997. Bred by Anna Kennedy he has King of Diamonds blood on both sides. His dam Grey Curragong (10604) is a daughter of The Conqueror by Flagmount Boy. He now holds US First and Second Level dressage certificates. He was placed 24th out of 1,666 horses competing at second level. He won three dressage championships and has been High Point once. He was launched on a showjumping career in 2002 under Rob Gage.

PHF Shanahoe

PHF Shanahoe is a 1995 son of Merry Mate out of the Kindgsway Diamond mare Lady Cooline. A chesnut he stands 16.2 hh. He is owned by Persimmon Hill Farm, 629 Wilson Road, Warrenton GA 30828

Ri an Domhan

Ri an Domhan (813) is a 1988 chesnut son of Golden Warrior (752) by Rathlin Star (707) by Armada Star (566). His dam is the Flagmount Boy mare Inch Lady Fair. He stood in Ireland with James McMahon in Co Clare and is owned by Orchard Hill Equestrian Centre.

Rockrimmon Silver Diamond

Rockrimmon Silver Diamond (846) is a 1994 son of Sillot Hill (735) by Slievenamon (682). Sillot Hill's dam Warren Lass (8719) was by Brandon Hill (517). Rockrimmon's dam was Saggart's Millie (11152) a daughter of Diamond Prince (726) by King of Diamonds. Her dam was Silver Candy an AID mare by Silver Hunter (681) He was bred by Patrick Gleeson. He is owned by Allen Stout, North Carolina. He was Approved in 2000 in Ireland.

Snowford Bellman

Snowford Bellman is a 1990 son of Slievenamon out of Snowford Harebell by Skippy. He was foaled in England and performance tested NASTA Grade 1 He is owned by Red Ridge Farm, 501 Swisher road, Crimora, VA 24431

The Irish Rover

The Irish Rover is a 1993 son of Kildalton Gold oput of the Pride of Shaunlara mare Knockavaher Pride. He was foaled in Ireland and is a chesnut standing 17.00 hh. He is owned by Normandy Farm, 409 Keller-Haslet Road, Keller, Texas 76248

The King of Hearts

The King of Hearts (861) is a 1994 bay son of Knave of Hearts (615) by King of Diamonds out of Cahir Beauty (10713) by King Elvis (708) by Pride of Shaunlara (636). He was bred and produced by Brendan Bradley, Eyrecourt, Co Galway. He was Approved in 2000.

Tors Gentleman Farmer

Tors Gentleman Farmer is a 1998 son of King Elvis out of Roma Forest Fox. He is a chesnut standing 16.1hh. He stands at Red Ridge Farm, 501 Swisher Road, Crimora VA 24431.

Touch of the Blues

Touch of the Blues 1987 black 16.3 by Blue Rajah (759) out of Seafin Lady (10309) by Slievenamon (682) bred by John and Sharyn Alexander, exported to UK and owned by John Brewster, Northallerton, North Yorkshire, sire of six stallion sons in Britain before being exported to USA. He is owned by Penmerryl Farm, PO Box 402, Greenvale VA 24440.

Touch of the Blues is the sire of the successful show hunter

Beamish 111 owned by Jane Warner and produced by David Bartram. Lady Megan and Summer Blues were also successful. Lady Megan was a winner at the Great Yorkshire on three occasions, similarly at Bridlington, and won several championships at the British national Irish Draught show. Summer Blues won a succession of show hunter classes and was Supreme champion at the 2001 British national breed show.

There is no doubt that Touch of the Blues is an exceptional stallion and had he stayed in Ireland would have done a great deal for Slievenamon although he might never have had the opportunities that his export to Great Britain and the USA have provided. He was bought in Dublin in 1987 as a foal by Archie Smith Maxwell who sold him to John Brewster of Garth Cottage Farm, Northallerton, North Yorkshire, who stood him until 1996 when he was sold to his new owners, Penmerryl Stud. While he was at stud with John Brewster he was broken and ridden by his daughter Jane Mogridge, who competed with him successfully at both eventing and dressage. He has produced over 125 individual champions who between them have won nearly 100 championships. John Brewster has two daughters and two grand daughters riding and competing young horses by Touch of the Blues.

Touch of the Blues was three times champion at Dublin Horse Show and twice champion at the Irish Draught national show. In the USA he was 1997 North American Grand champion He produced the 1998, 1999, and 2000 champion pure bred foals in North America and 2000 supreme champion. He is a NASTA Grade 1 performance tested stallion. He is the sire of Caerba Mac Moon a successful showjumper in Europe.

Rhythm and Blues

Rhythm and Blues, a 1998 stallion son of Touch of the Blues foaled in America, went to Germany in 2002 with his owner Dan Butler and successfully underwent the warmblood performance testing programme there Rhythm and Blues was Supreme Champion at the North American national ID breed show in 2000 and was unbeaten in in-hand classes. He took part in the 30 day state performance test at Marbach, near Stuttgart. Inspectors from the IDHS in Ireland travelled to Germany to insect the horse for the Irish Studbook. Efforts are being made to locate Irish Draughts exported to Germany around fifteen to twenty years ago to set up a German studbook for the breed.

Winmaur Sergeant Pepper

Winmaur Sergeant Pepper is a 1996 son of Snowford Bellman out of the Colman mare Snowford Bright Pink, a full sister of Snowford Stoker. He is a chesnut standing 15.1hh. He is owned by Penmerryl Farm. Greenvale VA. Winnmaur Sergeant Pepper was grade in Britain in 2000. He has tremendous presence with good paces and a neat scopey jump. His first foals were born in 2002. He was bred by Maggie Spreckley.

Stallions in Australia

Branigan's Pride

Branigan's Pride foaled 1985 was exported to Australia in 1988. He is a 16.3hh grey son of Pride of Shaunlara by Milestone out of Blue Hills. He is a Grade B showjumper and Medium dressage performer. He was bred by Marily Power, Suma Stud, Co Meath Blue Hills is a daughter of Blue Peter (536) out of Hill Cherry (8474) by Blackbird (583). His contact in Australia is Dr Robyn Woodward, Program Leader in Equine Studies, Roseworthy Campus, University of Adelaide.

Celtic Gold

Celtic Gold (838) foaled 1992 was exported to Australia in December 1997. He is a 16.2hh chesnut son of Kildalton Gold out of the Clover Hill mare Carnalway Lady (10758). He was bred by John Sandall, Co Kildare. He was national Irish Draught champion yearling in 1994 and was amongst the top performers in the 1995 Performance Test. He is owned by Jan Heine, Faraway Farm, Aura Vale road, Menzies Creek, Victoria, Australia 3159. In Ireland he was owned by Tom Meagher and Charles Hanley.

Coosheen Liam

Coosheen Liam foaled in 1987 was exported to Australia in 1997. He is a son of Colman (612) out of Coosheen Girl He is a bay standing 17.2 hh. He is owned by Tim and Penny Reeve, Mountmellick Stud, Tallarook, Victoria, Australia 3659.

Kilharkin

Kilharkin is a son of KIltoghert Casey out of Suma's Harkaway.

He was foaled in 1995. A grey he stands 17.1hh He is owned by Larry Greetham, The Celtic Stud, Gundaroo, New South Wales, Australia.

King's County

Kings County is a 1988 son of Holycross by Ben Purple out of the Slyguff Hero mare Madame Joy. He is a liver chesnut and stands 17 hands.He is owned by Michele Vasseur, Ballyshannon Lodge, Foggs Road, Mt Samson, Queensland, Australia 3659.

Stallions in New Zealand

Coalman's Touch

Coalman's Touch by Touch of the Blues out of the Colman mare Warrenhouse Blackbird was imported to New Zealand in 1998. He stands with Colin and Raewyn Price, Bush road, Oxford, North Canterbury, New Zealand.

Kingsway Diamond

Kingsway Diamond (736) was bred by Francesd Hatton out of the Dublin champion Bawnlahan Beauty. Foaled in 1980 he stood as a young sire with Thomas Niland in Co Mayo. Thady Ryan brought him out to New Zealand. He left two stallion sons behind in Ireland, Corran King (785) and Cream of Diamonds (780). Thady Ryan lives at Scarteen, 227 Te Awa Road, Temucka RD 25 New Zealand

The Future

Report on the Irish Draught Population in Ireland

A team of researchers, four from the Faculty of Agriculture, University College, Dublin, and one specialist from the Irish Horse Board reported to the Department of Agriculture in December 2001, that "the number of Irish Draught horses has now reached such a critical level that it is currently categorised as an endangered breed."

The research team, Helen O'Toole B.Agr. SC., Patrick Brophy MVB MRCVS, Dr Denis Kelleher, Lynn Aldridge M Agr.Sc., and Katherine Quinn, M. Agr. Sc, warned that if the Irish Draught horse population was to continue its role in present day breeding then it would have to be carefully managed as a rare genetic resource. The report said that increasing the population size was only part of the solution. The population had to remain genetically diverse if it was to survive in the longer term. The study suggested that conserving genetic diversity in the population could be helped by modifying some of the existing breeding practices. This included maintaining equal 'family' size giving each sire and dam an equal chance of breeding and contributing genetically to the population. The mating of related individuals should be avoided as much as possible to keep the coefficient of inbreeding low. The most difficult issue would probably be the need to increase the number of breeding males, and thereby increase the ratio of males to females which would help maintain genetic diversity.

This report, the first characterisation study to be made of the breed challenges the Irish authorities and breeders. The researchers are clearly correct in their assessment of the population decline, and given the market forces which govern horsebreeding, an organised conservation scheme could only be introduced if it was funded by either the Department of Agriculture or the Irish Horse Board.

While there may be many dedicated Irish Draught breeders, they cannot realistically be expected to breed foals which may not be financially viable in order to preserve genetic diversity or increase the population. Foals must have an intrinsic value which these days is based on performance pedigree. The fact that a particular stallion may have rare genes is not a justification for using him if he is not up to standard. Breeders must produce foals which can be moved on. The report correctly draws attention to the fact that the excellence of the Irish Draught in producing crossbred foals that are often of greater economic value than pure bred Irish Draught foals is the major factor that has led to a decrease in the numbers of pure bred Irish Draught horses.

The declared objective of the study was to evaluate how the genetic composition of the Irish Draught horse population in Ireland may have been affected by declining population numbers and past breeding practices. The study focused on a reference population of 1,317 Irish Draught horses registered with the Irish Horse Register, born between 1997 and 2000 inclusive. This population represents the future breeding stock of the Irish Draught horse. The pedigrees in the reference population were traced back to the last recorded ancestors. Additional pedigree for more distant relatives was provided by the pedigree records maintained by the Irish Draught Horse Society of Great Britain. When all records were included the pedigree data set contained 16,310 individual records.

The researchers defined two stages to the characterisation of the reference population. These were demographic and genetic. The demographic analysis described the reference population by total and change caused by the number of foals born. The demographic analysis also calculated the average generation interval and the average family size. This was measured by the number of offspring from each stallion and mare which were used for breeding.

The genetic analysis described the level of in breeding in the population. It also described the balance of contributions made by horses with one or two parents unknown which are described as founder horses, as well as the contribution of important ancestors and the contribution made by the Thoroughbred to the population.

Demographic Characterisation

In their demographic analysis of the reference population, the researchers found that there was a decline in the number of Irish Draught mares used for breeding. In 1997 804 Irish Draught mares including AID mares produced registered foals. In 2000 727 mares produced registered foals. The number of stallions involved over the period was 87, a figure which did not change significantly in any year.

There was a decline in the use of RID stallions on mares outside the Irish Draught studbook. The number of RID mares that produced foals by RID stallions increased from 239 in 1997 to 271 in 2000. The number of AID, ISH and thoroughbred mares that produced foals by RID stallions declined over the four year period by about 120 mares.

The number of purebred foals produced from 1997 to 2000 averaged 330 per year. The number of AID mares producing purebred foals declined from 92 in 1997 to 52 in 2000. The report observes that the contribution made by AID mares to the pure bred Irish Draught population is in decline as the number of AID mares approved under the Appendix scheme which operated from 1982 to 1993 had fallen.

Discussing the age profile of mares and stallions in the reference population, the researchers state that 11% of stallions were less than 8 years old when they sired foals, 72% were aged between 8 and 16 years and 17% were older. Five per cent of mares were less than five years old when they bred foals, 84% were aged between 5 and 16 years and 11% were over 17.

On family size the researchers say that each stallion in the pedigree produced 1.92 'breeding' male offspring and 5.84 'breeding' female offspring. Offspring were categorised as 'breeding' offspring if they produced at least one foal themselves. Sire family sizes were found to be unequal as 10% of the stallions produced just over 50% of the 'breeding' female and 30% of the 'breeding' male offspring. For example one stallion produced 69 breeding female offspring where as other stallions produced only one.

The report states that on average each mare in the pedigree produced 1.14 'breeding' male and 1.31 'breeding' female offspring. Family size in mares was found to be more equal than stallions due to the biological limitation of a mare to produce one foal naturally each year.

The average age of parents when their progeny were born was 11.65 years. This is described as the generation interval. The average age of sires was nearly three years longer than dams. The generation interval increased from 10.8 years in 1980 to 12.2 years in 2000.

Genetic Characterisation

Discussing the genetic characterisation of the Irish Draught reference population, the report says that as the research was based on pedigree records, the first step taken was the assessment of the quality of the information. Pedigree completeness was measured by what proportion of ancestors were known per generation. The pedigrees of the parents and grandparents were 100% complete. The great grandparents (generation 3) and great-great grandparents (generation 4) were 90% and 70% complete respectively. Pedigree information continued to decline and by generation 8 only 10% of the pedigree was recorded. The researchers comment that the pedigrees were considered moderately complete compared to other horse populations.

Discussing inbreeding the researchers found that there was a relatively low inbreeding co-efficient compared to some horse populations of similar population size. The co-efficient for the Irish Draughts was 0.86%. The coefficient of inbreeding measures the probability that an animal receives identical genes by descent from its sire and dam and so expresses the degree of relationship between an individual's parents. The average inbreeding coefficient increased by 0.499% from 1980 to 2000. The researchers state that this increase was less than one would expect in a population of this size under random mating. The low level of inbreeding in the Irish Draught, they say, may be due to the incomplete pedigree records or may be due to the deliberate avoidance of the mating of related individuals, or a combination of the two.

The researchers examined the number of 'founders' and 'ancestors' in the reference population. A founder is defined as an animal with both parents or one parent unknown. There were 1114 founder animals in the population. All the animals in the population are ultimately descended from these founders. Other things being equal the larger the number of founders the greater the genetic diversity would be expected amongst those founders. The greater the inequality of contribution amongst the founders to the reference population the greater is the risk of loss of genetic diversity through random drift and inbreeding. There were 135 'effective founders' in the reference population. The effective number of founders is the theoretical number that would produce a population with the same genetic diversity as the reference population if all the founders had contributed equally. The discrepancy between the actual number of founder animals (1114) and the effective number of founders (135) implies that not all the founder animals contributed equally to the reference population which would indicate a risk of losing genetic diversity.

Discussing ancestors, which differ from founders in that the pedigree may or may not be recorded, the researchers say that the most important ancestor was King of Diamonds who contributed 7.1% of the genes in the reference population. Ben Purple and Milestone were the next most important ancestors and each contributed over 5% of the genes in the reference population. Clover Hill featured as the next most important ancestor contributing over 3% of the genes. Overall 17 ancestors contributed 50% of the genes. As with the founder contributions, some ancestors contributed more genes than others, which could be a factor contributing to the risk of decreasing the genetic diversity in the population.

Discussing the contribution made to the Irish Draught by the thoroughbred the researchers found that thoroughbred genes accounted for 8.7% of the genes in the reference population. The contribution made by the thoroughbred to the Irish Draught population varied over a period of 70 years. In the Irish Draught horses born between 1927 and 1930, thoroughbred genes accounted for just over 3.5% of all the genes in that population. In 1947 to 195O thoroughbred genes accounted for only 0.6% of the genes. However, by 1977 -1980 thoroughbred genes accounted for up to 13% of the genes in that population. In 1979 the Irish Draught Horse Studbook was closed and since then non-Irish Draught horses have not been allowed into the population except under specific circumstances which would explain the gradual decrease in the contribution made by the thoroughbred.

This report which is the first scientific analysis of the state of the Irish Draught as a breed poses a number of complex issues for breeders and authorities alike. The researchers are quite clear in their main conclusion. The breed must be managed as a rare genetic resource. Such management will require an input of funding from the state and committittment and expertise from breeders. Immediately there are questions about expanding the genetic diversity of the national Irish Draught population. How can this be done. The immediate source of diversity is of course the outcross stallions which are few in number. The question must be asked are these stallions good enough to warrant breeder support in the numbers required to improve their contribution to the national gene pool? Whatever may be the pressure to improve genetic diversity, there is no case at all for breeding to sub-standard sires. The recent approval of two sons of the outcross performance sire Seacrest, Coolcronan Wood and Sir Rivie, offer opportunities of diversity plus performance. But these are only two sources.

Diversity from Outside the Studbook

Should diversity be gained from outside the studbook? The decline in the influence of the thoroughbred on the Irish Draught breed has been paralleled by a decline in the popularity of the Irish Draught as a source of performance. Is there a message here? Are the performance problems due to a loss of thoroughbred genes and should thoroughbred blood be deliberately introduced once more. The new AID scheme (2002) might reintroduce some thoroughbred backbreeding which is new but it would be a limited amount.

Is there a case for selecting a number of suitable thoroughbred sires known to produce jumpers and allowing them to be visited by a limited number of Irish Draught mares with a view to registering their filly progeny as AID mares or selecting a colt as an approved stallion. This would be a method of ensuring that proven performance blood was introduced. Such a move would be controversial, indeed widely unpopular, and the issue of performance from the thoroughbred is not clearcut. The Irish breeding industry as a whole is dissatisfied with the contribution currently being made by thoroughbreds to performance, but at the same time there are a handful of thoroughbred stallions with good performance records that could be used. The road has been travelled before. Clover Hill is a good example of a colt by a thoroughbred stallion becoming an important contributor to the breed. The re-opening of the studbook along these lines should at least be considered. It may well be that there is no other option. If there is not enough performance and diversity currently within the breed then it is surely necessary to go outside the studbook and admit a limited number of colts from RID mares by proven thoroughbred sires.

The need for action is clear enough. There are less than 2000

Irish Draughts world wide. This study is very specific. Numbers have declined in recent years and the Irish Draught is classified as an endangered breed. In what other ways might the future of the breed be secured. Is there a case for granting premiums for mares to go to selected stallions, increasing the population numbers, and at the same time ensuring that the best sires are supported. But is there a market for an increase in the number of purebred foals born each year. What is to be done with them.

If Irish Draught fillies had good enough performance, sport horse breeders generally would favour them as brood mares. It is perhaps a fair enough comment to make that since the breed as a whole is getting lighter, the physical gap between the RID mare and the ISH mare will not be that marked in years to come. Irish Draught breeders could work themselves out of their bind if they could produce fillies which had a high degree of athleticism as well as substance and bone. A marketing goal could surely be the encouragement of sport horse breeders to utilise suitable types of purebred fillies as their brood mares. Performance is the key to this. Without it, the Irish Draught filly will go nowhere as a suitable brood mare for the general horse breeder. Such an approach would of course involve a changed outlook on the part of breeders whose vision of a broodmare is generally one of substance and weight.

Goal Must be to Improve Performance

The goal must be to improve performance in the breed and encourage more sport horse breeders to use purebred mares. For this to be achieved, the fillies will have to have the attributes of the better type of sport horse mare. Inevitably this will lead to a lighter, more athletic type of Irish Draught filly, but the breed is lightening anyway. Traditional bone and substance may be an ideal, but in the horse world of the future, bone will be of secondary consideration. An ability to jump, stay sound, and have a good brain and temperament are the qualities that will be sought in all horses. The Irish Draught if it could get over the performance hurdles is uniquely placed to provide such qualities.

There is no point in genetically and demographically managing a breed that has no place in the scheme of things. The modern equestrian world has its own process of evolution. The Irish Draught can maintain its place as one of the important steps in that evolution only if it evolves itself. There is no future in building up numbers in fields going nowhere. Performance is the key to survival. If the Irish Draught world truly grasped this fact it could make the future of the breed secure for all time. Achievement of this aim, of course, is more easily spoken about than done.

The Irish Draught as a breed needs a partner in its battle for survival. That partner is unquestionably the thoroughbred horse, the great improver of all breeds. Genetic diversity and greater numbers will be achieved by careful use of the opportunities which the thoroughbred world provides. The thoroughbred lies behind the Irish Draught performance bloodlines. King of Diamonds, and more lately Clover Hill, owe as much to their thoroughbred backgrounds as to the Irish Draught in their pedigree. Surely it is no coincidence that the fortunes of the Irish Draught as a breed have waned in tandem with the decline in the extent of their thoroughbred genes.

While the concept of a closed studbook and concentration on the ongoing registration of only purebred stock is a laudable ideal, it has already been breached in recent times. The registration of stallions with up to 50% thoroughbred blood has been a feature of the studbook from time to time in the past. As pointed out before the registration of Clover Hill, the son of the racehorse Golden Beaker, is a case in point. It is arguable that the Irish Draught might have already vanished from the scene had it not been for the lifegiving legacies of King of Diamonds and Clover Hill. The AID scheme opened the studbook and the IDHS in 2001 reiterated this approach by developing its new AID scheme which was launched in 2002.

The concept of genetic management at its most basic implies the use of little used stallions to maintain genetic diversity. The reason why certain stallions are not supported by breeders is that they are deemed to be sub standard, either in terms of conformation or performance. A management policy that calls for the support of such sires just because they have rare bloodlines is one which can only be self defeating. The old breeding rule of the best to the best still applies. Breeders have ignored these stallions because they are not up to scratch. A genetic management policy will have to be applied by utilising stallions which have credentials to be sires. Otherwise their progeny have no value.

It is a difficult situation and one which can only be resolved by bold decisions. Where can the Irish Draught acquire more genetic diversity? It can only come from outside the breed, and the only acceptable source is the thoroughbred. The thoroughbred blood that is used can only be performance blood and that in fact makes the job much simpler because there are only a handful of approved thoroughbred sires that can be nominated for the role. The difficulty facing the breed can be simply summarised. It must go for performance. Performance is the lifeline, there is no other solution. If it cannot be produced from within the breed at the present time, then the old and trusted and acceptable standby, the thoroughbred, must be called into service again.

Brood Mare Herd Survey

The Breeding committee of the Irish Draught Horse Society carried out a survey of the Brood Mare Herd in 2001. The committee said that it was of the opinion that the breed was in a similar position to that of the mid to late eighties. The Breeding Committee was concerned at the decline in the number of Irish Draught mares at stud, the proportion being bred pure and the extremely low registration rate. The report reviewed the breeding trends of the past fifteen to twenty years

The Breeding commitee observed that the Irish Draught herd is made up of Registered Irish Draught (RID) mares and Appendix Irish Draught (AID) mares. The herd size increased from 748 in 1986 to a peak of 1755 in 1993. Since 1993 the number has declined steadily. The number of RID mares at stud has remained fairly constant, however, and has averaged 700 since 1990. In 1993 there was an all time high of 992. In 1999 there were 677 RID mares at stud of which 360 or 53% were covered by RID sires. In the same year there were 315 AID mares at stud of which 82 or 26% were covered by RID sires.

Appendix Mare Scheme

The Appendix Irish Draught scheme began in 1982 and continued for eleven years. The last mares were registered in 1992. Over the years approximately 1266 mares were registered as AID. The objectives of the scheme were to increase the number of RID mares in view of the fact that the number of mares was below the level need to increase future numbers. Filly foals by RID stallions out of AID mares were eligible for RID registration. The committee found that the overall increase and decline in the mare herd was due to changes in the number of AID mares at stud since the number of pure bred mares had remained constant. Out of 1658 mares registered as RID since 1982, 488 were produced by AID mares The committee observed that quality improvement was difficult to quantify. However it pointed to the fact that 25% of the Irish Draught mares approved for the Irish Horse Board's Quality Broodmare Retention Scheme were AID mares.

In September 2001, the IDHS met with the Irish Horse Board and agreed that the Appendix Register should be re-opened on a very limited basis. The IDHS stipulated that that applicant mares should have one RID parent and three RID grandparents. The scheme was to be reviewed after one year. In a move designed to scoop up purebred but unregistered mares the IDHS also decided to introduce a special measure. The new scheme, the Amnesty Registration scheme offered registration to mares whose pedigree was verified as full Irish Draught for two generations. The society observed that there were mares in the national herd which were Irish Draught but which could not be registered because their dams had not been registered. These moves should increase the registered population somewhat but it is questionable whether many mares will be garnered from the Amnesty Scheme. The society widened its net somewhat with an offer that older mares could be registered free of charge provided they met the normal registration criteria. The numbers which might come in under the new AID scheme are perhaps a more promising prospect given that over twelve hundred mares were registered over the eleven years of the scheme. However, the new scheme would presumably have to operate for a similar timespan to achieve the necessary numbers.

Incentive Schemes

Discussing the effect of the Irish Draught Horse Incentive Scheme which ran from 1990 to 1984 under which a grant of £400 was paid to the breeder of each live pure bred foal, the commitee found that the significant increase in the number of mares at stud began the year before the commencement of the scheme and declined from the last year of the scheme. The number of RID mares at stud increased by 24% in the four years after the scheme. The successful RID mares under the Quality Brood Mare Retention scheme from 1995 to 1999 numbered 290, 24.74% of the total. Almost 50% (572) mares accepted were by RID stallions. It is thought that many of the remainder were out of RID and AID mares. The IDHS has asked the Horse Board to back a scheme allowing a grant of £200 for pure bred foals. Mares accepted for the Quality Brood Mare Scheme or the Premier Brood mare scheme would be eligible as would mares accepted for the new premier brood mare scheme.

Registrations

Discussing the annual registration of brood mares the Breeding Committee found that the number of RID mares accepted for registration in 2000 at 165 was the best result for over a decade. The acceptance rate was 83.61% The committee found that only 39% of the filly foals born annually from AID and RID mares are subsequently registered as RID. Breeders can present their fillies for registration at any age over two years The committee found that the average stud life of a mare is seven years. The average number of foals produced per RID mare is 3.79. These figures are based on random sampling of the Irish Draught Mare book published by the Irish Horse Board.

If in fact the stud life of most mares is as short as seven years there is considerable scope for increasing it. As is shown in the section on Special Mares in this book, Irish Draught mares can produce fifteen and more foals in their lives. One must conclude that for whatever reason, many breeders are not getting the best out of their mares. The Irish Draught like the Connemara pony is fertile, fecund and long lived. Management of the mare is, of course, a vital part of breeding. Breeders should avail of veterinary asistance to ensure that their mares are clean and maintain them adequately in the winter months to ensure a productive breeding season year on year.

There is clearly scope for increasing breed numbers with a campaign to encourage greater registration of purebred fillies. The issue of getting more purebred mares in foal to breed stallions is much more complex. The fact that only just over 50% of mares are covered by RID stallions raises serious questions, not just about the standard of stallions but about the viability of a breeder engaging in the production of purebred stock.

If more sport horse breeders could be encouraged to use RID fillies as brood mares the future of the breed would be much less in doubt. There would be a market and more foals would be produced. But the Irish Draught mare will only come to be accepted as a general brood mare by sport horse breeders if there is a strong performance bias. There is hope. Young Irish Draught performance stallions have now come on stream and they should soon be producing fillies with special ability. Some of these stallions have already found favour with purebred breeders. Crosstown Dancer and Huntingfield Rebel have established reputations but they are being closely challenged by the younger up and coming sires such as Finn's Clover Inn, Mount Diamond Flag, Star Kingdom, Sir Rivie and All the Diamonds.

These are stallions of the performance testing era and they should bring something special in terms of athleticism to the breed. As more and more young stallions come through the system, the image of the Irish Draught as a performance breed should improve. If we can get to the stage when an Irish Draught filly is rated as acceptable to sport horse breeders as the current sport horse broodmare then the future will be more secure. The same could be said for the stallions. If the performance tested Irish Draught sires can match the performance abilities of the sport horse stallions, then breeders will use them in greater numbers.

The key to the future is performance and anyone who refuses to recognise the fact is living in the nineteenth century. Performance will give the Irish Draught a lifeline to the future. King of Diamonds and Clover Hill put the Irish Draught on the map in their day. Surely there are other stallions coming on stream which can do the same for the new generation. While these performance tested stallions have potential will they really solve the breed's problems. The question must be asked: Is there enough performance currently within the breed to sustain it in the future? My personal belief is that there is not. The Irish Draught needs a top up to put in an equal footing with the sport horse and foreign challengers. There is only one way to in search of quality and performance - the thoroughbred.

Back to the Thoroughbred

The proposition that the Irish Draught as a breed must look again to the thoroughbred as the source of quality, performance and survival will not be a popular suggestion. But the situation in which the breed finds itself is clear enough. It will not survive unless steps are taken to increase numbers and genetic diversity. There is only one route. The thoroughbred has always been the guardian angel of the Irish Draught horse whether breeders and enthusiasts like it or not. It is to the thoroughbred that the Irish Draught will have to turn to for survival. Peformance is the key element. The Irish Draught must evolve to at least challenge the other breeds. Breeders and enthusiasts will have to accept the changes in substance and bone that such a move entails, but the very special attributes of the Irish Draught, temperament, action, conformation, and brain, will not be affected by the addition of thoroughbred genes.

At the end of the day what is looked for in the Irish Draught as a breed is the continuance of its role as a riding horse. It has no option but to meet the changing demands of the modern equestrian world. By facing up to these demands, breeders will ensure that the Irish Draught will be around in the years to come. At this point in time, however, there is not sufficient performance within the breed to ensure its survival in the years ahead. Some stallions have been able to reach Grade A but they do not go any further. The majority of stallions do not have the athletic ability to go even this far. But if Grade A was set as the minimum standard for stallion approval the breed would at least be pointed in the right direction. Can this be achieved without the addition of thoroughbred performance. I doubt it.

To close this book it might not be out of place to refer to the Irish Draughts which have displayed the prowess and courage that demonstrates that there is within the breed a great reservoir of natural ability which must be exploited whether or not the thoroughbred route is travelled again. There is the Grand Prix showjumping star Coille Mor Hill, winner of more than thirty competitions. There is Grange Bouncer proving himself an adept performer both in showjumping and eventing.

The newly approved stallion Sir Rivie is well on his way as an outstanding showjumper. The gelding Kingman is building up a reputation in eventing. In dressage the mare Breezes Sue is proving a polished performer.

In the showing world, Billy Cotter's Enniskeane Flash dominated at Limerick and Dublin. Crosstown Dancer pulled off a remarkable double at Dublin Horse Show 2001 when his progeny won the Pembroke Cup and reserve.

Ireland has had a stupendous run of success on the Nations Cup circuit. Five of the thirteen horses that represented Ireland in these competitions were by RID stallions. Coolcorron Cool Diamond featured in three Nations Cup victories.

These up to the minute achievements show that despite its problems the Irish Draught is entitled to be highly valued by the Irish horse industry. That the breed faces a challenging and difficult future is clear enough. Given the will to take bold decisions this national asset can be brought back from the brink. The modern Irish Draught is not the horse of yesterday. The breed is changing. There is no point in lamenting for the past. Horse breeding in the twentyfirst century is about evolution. These are changing times. The Irish Draught must change to meet them.